SOCIAL & EMOTIONAL CURRICULUM FOR GIFTED STUDENTS

SOCIAL & EMOTIONAL CURRICULUM FOR GIFTED STUDENTS

Grade 4

Project-Based Learning Lessons That Build Critical Thinking, Emotional Intelligence, and Social Skills

Mark Hess

PRUFROCK PRESS INC.
WACO, TEXAS

Copyright ©2021, Prufrock Press Inc.

Edited by Stephanie McCauley

Cover and layout design by Shelby Charette

ISBN-13: 978-1-64632-115-5

No part of this book may be reproduced, translated, stored in a retrieval system, or transmitted, in any form or by any means, electronic, mechanical, photocopying, microfilming, recording, or otherwise, without written permission from the publisher.

Prufrock Press grants the individual purchasing this book permission to photocopy original activity pages for single classroom use. This permission does not include electronic reproduction rights. Should you wish to make copies of materials we sourced or licensed from others, request permission from the original publisher before reproducing that material.

For more information about our copyright policy or to request reprint permissions, visit https://www.prufrock.com/permissions.aspx.

Printed in the United States of America.

At the time of this book's publication, all facts and figures cited are the most current available; all telephone numbers, addresses, and website URLs are accurate and active; all publications, organizations, websites, and other resources exist as described in this book; and all have been verified. The author and Prufrock Press make no warranty or guarantee concerning the information and materials given out by organizations or content found at websites, and we are not responsible for any changes that occur after this book's publication. If you find an error or believe that a resource listed here is not as described, please contact Prufrock Press.

Prufrock Press Inc.
P.O. Box 8813
Waco, TX 76714-8813
Phone: (800) 998-2208
Fax: (800) 240-0333
https://www.prufrock.com

Table of Contents

Introduction — 1

Unit 1: Superheroes: Perfectionism and Self-Understanding — 5

    Lesson 1.1: Superhero Commercials — 8
    Lesson 1.2: Superhero Abilities — 11
    Lesson 1.3: Saving the Day With Superpowers — 15
    Lesson 1.4: Engineering Design Challenge — 22
    Lesson 1.5: The Grappling Hook Metaphor — 27
    Lesson 1.6: Perfectionism Shield — 33
    Lesson 1.7: Sidekicks — 39

Unit 2: Spy Training: Self-Esteem — 45

    Lesson 2.1: Understanding Self-Esteem — 48
    Lesson 2.2: Internalizing Positive Self-Esteem: Dead Drops — 57
    Lesson 2.3: Creating a Legend and Case File — 63
    Lesson 2.4: What's in Your Pockets? — 69
    Lesson 2.5: Award Certificate and Diary — 76

Unit 3: Antibullying Intervention: Empathy and Justice — 81

    Lesson 3.1: Antibullying Inventions — 84
    Lesson 3.2: Preparing an Antibullying Speech — 88
    Lesson 3.3: Delivering the Antibullying Speech — 92

Unit 4: Penguin Problems: Ownership and Accountability — 95

    Lesson 4.1: Penguin Problems — 98
    Lesson 4.2: Penguin Problem as a Metaphor — 101
    Lesson 4.3: Penguin Solutions — 107
    Lesson 4.4: Gratitude: Listen to the Walrus — 112

Social and Emotional Curriculum for Gifted Students Grade 4

Unit 5: Our Colorful Selves: Personality and Giftedness	**117**
Lesson 5.1: Drawing With a Compass	120
Lesson 5.2: Overlapping Circles	122
Lesson 5.3: What Colors Are You?	125
Lesson 5.4: Blending Colors	131
Lesson 5.5: Making Connections With Tangents	135
Lesson 5.6: What Color Is Giftedness?	141
Conclusion: Dear Gifted Learner	**145**
References	**159**
About the Author	**161**

Introduction

The process of growing into one's wonderful self can be messy. The most meaningful pathways don't follow a straight line. The social and emotional lives of gifted children are wide and deep, and the journey toward self-understanding is the most essential part of teaching and learning.

Yet educators tend to think of the social-emotional aspects of giftedness as issues to be addressed, problems to overcome, or roadblocks to thriving. In moments of frustration, as teachers and parents, we might forget about one of the most essential components of giftedness—asynchronous development. Just because a gifted 6-year-old can think like a 10-year-old doesn't mean that same student should have developed the social skills of a 10-year-old. The 6-year-old, in fact, may have the social skills of a 4-year-old. Little kids with little hands may envision an engineering project well beyond their years but may not be able to handle scissors well or know how to use drafting tools or design software. These frustrations abound in the asynchronous world of gifted learners, yet these frustrations are both common and normal. We might stumble into a deficit model of thinking about these asynchronous challenges.

In these moments, I hope we don't forget the beauty of intensities—the way gifted learners tend to experience the world in a more rich and textured way, are able to make connections others cannot, and are able to create a personal poetry in this world if we only stop and listen to them. I hope we don't forget about the value of the journey itself. The lessons and units in this book offer an engaging variety of pathways for students to share their journey with teachers and with one another.

Background

I first taught elementary gifted kids in a small school district at the foot of Pikes Peak. My classroom was in the 1923 wing of the original school building. Eight-foot high windows looked out on Colorado's Front Range. The oak floor was the original floor from 1923, stained and sealed many times over into a rich brown, with black dots in perfect lines where the desks had once been bolted in place. A former second-grade teacher's name was etched into the slate blackboard in a beautiful, swooping, cursive script.

The gifted groups who came bounding down the stairs to my classroom, however, were anything but bolted in place. We worked with craft saws and hot glue, piles of cardboard, nuts and bolts, small pieces of wood, batteries, wires, and switches. We made trash bag bat wings, plaster bear paw prints created in the mud outside, marshmallow trebuchets, miniature skate parks, and an elf village populated by peanut people dressed in felt clothing. This was STEAM curriculum before anyone had used that term. This was creative graphic design when the most complicated design program available to us was Kid Pix. I remember reading learning standards from the National Association for Gifted Children (NAGC) for the first time during these years, and I thought they rang true, but the standards didn't guide my teaching. Instead, I drove to a recycling center and filled my truck with 2-liter soda bottles so my class could duct tape together a tube that would carry a tennis ball all around the room, allowing it to roll from ceiling to floor. I spent my planning time not wondering how my students would learn more about themselves as gifted learners, but dreaming up the next thematic unit and the next project.

Teaching and loving these kids helped me understand that being gifted goes far beyond creative expression and passion projects. Giftedness often means leading with the heart. My students tended to lead with their kindness and compassion, were guided by a full range of feelings and emotions, and were often very hard on themselves. Emotional intensity in the gifted is, as Sword (2011) so poetically described, "vivid, absorbing, penetrating, encompassing, complex, commanding—a way of being quaveringly alive" (para. 3). Many of our gifted students carry a reservoir of compassion. Their storehouse has been filled by an ability to see another's perspective and to imagine another's struggle. At a young age, our gifted students begin to sort out injustices and develop a beautiful acceptance of others. This reservoir of compassion, like no other, characterizes who gifted children are and sets the course for this book.

Development of Social-Emotional Units

When my students skip, run, and sometimes even walk appropriately through my classroom doorway, they expect exciting and engaging opportunities. That's why I believe approaching the vital social-emotional components of gifted programming should **never feel like a trip to the counseling office**. I want to use my best teacher skills and surprise students with vibrant experiences around social-emotional understanding—experiences that are often necessarily hands-on and creative.

Some of the lessons in this book did not begin as social-emotional lessons at all but grew out of curricular projects. Some grew out of conversations with parents, students, or classroom teachers. Some grew from a perceived need, an article I was writing, or a presentation for colleagues.

Unit 1: Superheroes: Perfectionism and Self-Understanding was crafted around the idea of superhero sidekicks. The most socially strong students I teach all seem to share the ability to laugh at themselves and to own their wonderful quirkiness. Wouldn't it be amazing to have a sidekick to support us in life and to help us own our quirky behaviors . . . to remind us not to take everything so seriously . . . to gently nudge us into accepting that we are not perfect, nor should we expect ourselves to be? This person could also lend us the confidence of fashion, because a sidekick, after all, is usually costumed even more ridiculously than the superhero.

Unit 2: Spy Training: Self-Esteem was born from this question: What is a topic fourth graders would find really cool? These lessons were a big hit in my classroom and have since blossomed into a full semester-long, cross-curricular unit with physics, research, engineering, graphic design, and even memory games collected within.

Unit 3: Antibullying Intervention: Empathy and Justice originated from a reading in my classroom. After reading Norma Fox Mazer's short story "Tuesday of the Other June," my gifted students' sense of justice hit peak levels. They were incensed by the bullying June had endured. I hoped, however, they would think about both sides of bullying—not only what it feels like to be bullied but also where a bully's motivation might originate. The lessons in Unit 3 helped meet this critical thinking exercise.

Unit 4: Penguin Problems: Ownership and Accountability encourages students to recognize when problems are not really problems at all. Gifted kids are just like other kids in many ways. My class was not immune to crises over "She swiped my pencil!," "He's copying me!" or, "Hey, I was first!" We, too, suffer our "penguin problems," and these lessons became a fun way to address them.

Several teachers with whom I've shared Unit 5: Our Colorful Selves: Personality and Giftedness have praised the unit's metaphorical potential, and it has become even more poignant in present times. The unit, however, grew from a very literal practice activity: learning how to draw circles with a compass (an important tool in an engineering classroom). You may have forgotten that this skill does not come easily to students. Little hands and slick paper make for a frustrating process. As I walked around the desks encouraging students as they practiced, I found myself talking about resilience and perfectionism and the right to be gifted and imperfect at the same time. One more social-emotional lesson was born.

Social and Emotional Curriculum for Gifted Students Grade 4

Teaching the Units

So how can teachers make the most profound impact in the short amount of time we have with our students? How can we engage creativity, stretch academic standards, and grow at the same time? Let's put our hearts and hands into cross-curricular projects designed to meet gifted students' thirst for self-expression. Let's provide opportunities for students to understand themselves a little better in each lesson. Each unit in this book begins with an active Launch lesson to engage gifted learners. Each unit is aligned to NAGC's (2019) Pre-K–Grade 12 Gifted Programming Standards, specifically the student outcomes from Standard 1: Learning and Development. Also included with each unit is a list of social-emotional themes addressed, as well as academic skills that will be enhanced.

I hope that you will weave these lessons in and out of your curriculum in a way that is personal to you and the children you teach. Please feel free to add, delete, or adjust to make these lessons your own. I hope that the process of growing into one's wonderful self is messy with hot glue, glitter, craft sticks, and construction paper, as well as with understanding. I hope that you and your students have as much fun and produce as many memories as mine have.

For even more engaging units for gifted learners, see the companion books in this series, *Social and Emotional Curriculum for Gifted Students: Grade 3* and *Social and Emotional Curriculum for Gifted Students: Grade 5*.

UNIT 1

Superheroes
Perfectionism and Self-Understanding

Background

If teachers were superheroes—and some days it seems we are, with both virtuosities and foibles—we would demand engaging hands-on activities, metaphors, critical thinking, art, and creativity for our very own social-emotional units. We will not disappoint with this unit.

The superheroes in this unit will teach gifted learners about perfectionism (a big issue for such amazing beings as superheroes); recognizing their own talents, abilities, and positive attitudes; friendship; and finally, not taking themselves too seriously.

Unit Objectives

Students will:
» recognize their strongest talents and abilities,
» identify people and ideas who support them, and
» address perfectionist tendencies.

Social and Emotional Curriculum for Gifted Students Grade 4

NAGC Learning and Development Standard

1.1. Self-Understanding. Students with gifts and talents demonstrate self-knowledge with respect to their interests, strengths, identities, and needs in socio-emotional development and in intellectual, academic, creative, leadership, and artistic domains.

Themes and Skills Addressed

Social-Emotional Themes
- » Effort
- » Humility
- » Growth mindset
- » Perfectionism
- » Friendship
- » Identity

Academic Skills
- » Inferences
- » Collaborative discussion
- » Metaphor analysis
- » Metaphor creation
- » Graphic design
- » Building and engineering
- » Improvisation

Launch

Launch the unit by showing the following Hotstar commercial about superheroes: https://www.youtube.com/watch?v=s-W3himDkwY. This commercial is not in English, and interpreting its meaning through the characters' actions, gestures, movements, and other sorts of nonverbal communication is an excellent critical thinking activity in and of itself.

After the students' first viewing of the commercial, discuss the following as a class:
- » What did you notice? List details. (No inferences here; let's save those for later.)
- » What stands out?
- » Who are the superheroes in this commercial, and what are their superpowers?

Before a second viewing, present the following prompts for students to consider as they watch:
- » *Situational irony* is when one thing happens, but we had expected something else to happen. List and explain ways that situational irony is used in this commercial.
- » What are the superheroes actually saying to one another?

Unit 1: Superheroes

After a second viewing, invite students to consider the answers to these questions in a small group or in pairs. Then come together as a full group to discuss the questions. End the discussion with this final question:
» Some people say that we all have a little superhero inside of us. Does this commercial support that view? Explain.

To extend the launch further, ask students to describe another superhero. How might that superhero be using their superpower in an extended version of the commercial?

Lesson 1.1

Superhero Commercials

How will Dead Battery Boy advertise umbrellas? Wait—what and who?

This is a creative and quick lesson that will engage students right away. Superheroes must be very resourceful, and our gifted learners can be, too. Equipped with only three craft sticks, a foot of tape, five notecards, and some unlikely superheroes matched to random products, can our superheroes-in-training create and perform a commercial?

Materials

- » Handout 1.1: Superhero Commercial
- » Commercial materials (per small group of 3–4 students)
    - » 3 craft sticks
    - » 1 foot of masking tape
    - » 5 notecards

Estimated Time

- » 20 minutes to introduce and complete the creative activity. Live performances of students' commercials will vary depending on the size of the class. These performances are meant to be quick and improvisational, not planned and perfected.

Procedure

Arrange students into groups of 3 or 4. Distribute commercial materials and Handout 1.1: Superhero Commercial to each group.

Launch right into the creative commercial activity. The final product is a commercial that students may perform for the class. Do not supply additional details or materials. If students ask questions, simply refer them back to the activity's guidelines. Part of the challenge and creative task is to work with ambiguity, trust oneself, and let go of perfectionism. Similarly, invite students to share their performances without additional rehearsal time. The commercials are intended to be improvisational and far from perfect—which is both part of the fun and part of the social-emotional lesson here.

For an extension activity, you might suggest that students create a video for their commercial and add background music. I do not. In my experience, filming and editing a video can be a long and sometimes frustrating process for fourth graders—sometimes a little obsessive, too, and worthy of a whole unit in and of itself. Students can get forever bogged down in the details of filming, rehearsals, writing scripts, and creating props.

The key takeaway from this lesson is that all students have a little superhero inside of them. Specifically, tell students: *This commercial creative task was demanding and had to be completed under time constraints, but just look at all of the little heroic efforts that went into the final product! Our creative responses were created from deep inside, and we followed through with entertaining performances. Just like a superhero, we came through in the clutch.*

NAME: _____ DATE: _____

Handout 1.1
Superhero Commercial

Directions: With your group members, choose a superhero and make a commercial advertising a product featuring that superhero. You have 15 minutes to create your commercial.

Choose One Superhero:	**Make the Commercial:**
» Dead Battery Boy » Sniffles Girl » Too Many Hats Guy » Lady Toothpaste	Make a commercial that is 30 seconds or less advertising one of the following products featuring the superhero you have chosen: » Dog food » Umbrellas » Breakfast cereal » Yard care » Used cars » Jewelry
Create a Prop: Create a prop or props from the materials provided. These are the only props allowed in the commercial. Materials include: » 3 craft sticks » 1 foot of masking tape » 5 notecards	**Heroic Bonus Challenge:** Add a jingle to the commercial!

Lesson 1.2

Superhero Abilities

In this lesson, students cite their strengths, both inside and outside of school. Students also note the vital ideas and behaviors that help them succeed. In a perspective-taking activity, students also think about how others perceive them—noting what strengths friends and family would likely recognize.

Materials

- » Handout 1.2: Superhero Possibilities
- » Handout 1.2: Superhero Possibilities Sample

Estimated Time

- » 15 minutes

Procedure

Distribute Handout 1.2: Superhero Possibilities for students to complete individually. Completing this brainstorming sheet may be the most difficult task of the unit. Students who are perfectionistic or modest may struggle to generate a list of their strongest skills and abilities. Encourage them to be honest with themselves. What qualities are they proud of? Explain to students that this is not bragging. Sample answers are provided on the page following the handout.

Some students may feel it is unsavory to list their strongest abilities, and others may not know where to stop. For both possibilities, share the "Dear Superhero" note in Figure 1. This note about humility may be helpful for those students who don't know where to stop, but it

Figure 1
Dear Superhero Letter

Dear superhero,

Being humble means being so confident and proud that you don't have to tell anyone about it.

Sincerely,

Your teacher

also says, "Hey, it's OK to be proud and confident about your abilities as long as you don't go around tooting your own horn." Discuss this quote with students to help clarify the rest of the lessons in this unit. Explain: *In this activity, we really do want to share our abilities, but we're doing it by invitation . . . quite humbly.*

A Note About Perfectionists. This exercise is valuable for perfectionists. Intercept any "yes, but" comments from students about themselves—for example, "I am good at math, but I am not very good at writing." Tell these students: *We are concentrating on A-bilities here, not INA-bilities. We are not interested to hear was comes after the word "but."*

Students will look more closely at perfectionism in Lesson 1.6 when they make their perfectionist "shields."

NAME:_____ DATE: _____

Handout 1.2
Superhero Possibilities

Directions: Any superhero needs to understand their greatest strengths and qualities. We can't have Aquaman trying to scale tall buildings like Spiderman, or Batgirl trying to fly an invisible jet like Wonder Woman! We all have different skills and abilities. Which ones are yours? *This isn't bragging*—not if you don't go around making announcements over the intercom, so be honest.

What I'm good at outside of school:

Ideas and behaviors I have that have helped me succeed:

What I'm good at in school:

What my friends or family would say I'm good at:

NAME:_____   DATE: _____

Handout 1.2

Superhero Possibilities Sample

Directions: Any superhero needs to understand their greatest strengths and qualities. We can't have Aquaman trying to scale tall buildings like Spiderman, or Batgirl trying to fly an invisible jet like Wonder Woman! We all have different skills and abilities. Which ones are yours? *This isn't bragging*—not if you don't go around making announcements over the intercom, so be honest.

What I'm good at outside of school:
Writing, playing the piano, and listening.

Ideas and behaviors I have that have helped me succeed:
Patience, being positive, being funny, and listening.

What I'm good at in school:
Crafting and cooking.

What my friends or family would say I'm good at:
Drawing and crafting.

Lesson 1.3

Saving the Day With Superpowers

In this lesson, students build metaphors—internalizing their thoughts about ideas, skills, attitudes, and abilities that benefit them the most. Students then represent those aspects in a physical product. We will help students engage both hemispheres of their brains in this way and enhance their learning experience. Crafting superpower metaphors is simply fun, too.

Hands on hips and standing proudly before the world, our student superheroes proclaim, "Hark! What's that I see? A challenge to be met? A problem to be addressed?" Raising a forearm, our students pop open their utility bracelets. "Allow me!" they chuckle confidently, brandishing awe-inspiring superhero gadgets, "No need to worry. I've got this!"

Materials

- » Handout 1.3: Utility Bracelet Superpowers
- » Handout 1.3: Utility Bracelet Superpowers Sample
- » Cardstock of various colors (several sheets per student): Cardstock is an excellent way to craft items because it is much easier to cut and shape than cardboard.
- » Small, empty boxes used to hold transparent tape (one per student)
- » Pipe cleaners (at least one per student)
- » Various craft items or junk drawer items (e.g., small plastic parts, small plastic animals or action figures, keyrings, small electronic parts—anything that could be used as an interesting part of a miniature craft item)

Estimated Time

- » At least 60 minutes—allow plenty of time.

Preparation

Start saving small boxes of tape. I asked teachers to save them for me at the start of the school year and gathered a big collection, which could last me 2 years or more; however, you can find a shortcut for building your collection of empty boxes by talking to the keeper of your school's supply closet. Mine allowed me to open all of the tape boxes in the supply closet and leave the tape behind. Who needs those boxes anyway?

Procedure

Explain that students are about to create miniature gadgets that will help them enact their superpowers. Similar to Batman and Batgirl, who have superhero utility belts, each student will create a utility bracelet. Students will construct this bracelet from a small box used to hold transparent tape, so the gadgets will need to be miniaturized to fit inside the small box (see examples in Figure 2).

Then, distribute the planning sheet, Handout 1.3: Utility Bracelet Superpowers, to help students transform their ideas into physical metaphors. Students will choose two skills or personal qualities that they might like to stow away in their bracelets. They will then brainstorm what gadgets or tools might represent their qualities and design a diagram or picture of one of the gadgets.

Once students have completed their planning and designs—creating "gadget" metaphors for their strongest qualities and skills—they will be begin crafting the small superhero gadget or tool that will fit inside the utility bracelets. When finished, students will proudly display their individual talents, symbolized by the amazing gadgets they've created to help them meet life's challenges.

Later, students will finish the utility bracelet by adding a grappling hook (see Lesson 1.5).

Unit 1: Superheroes

Figure 2
Utility Bracelet Item Examples

The Super Focus Force Field generated by this electronic grid projector allows for steady focus and achievement even during the most trying of times.

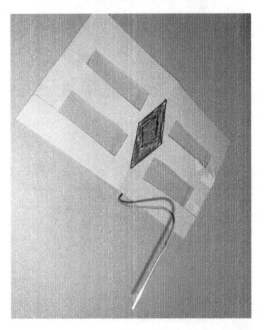

Never feel lost or out of place. Find your way and reset your direction and goals with this little electronic device.

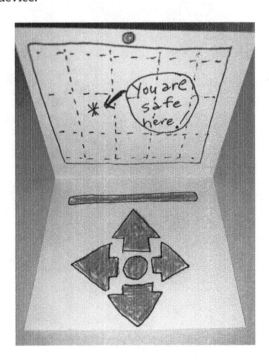

Figure 2, continued

Those aren't any old connectors. They're special universal connectors that allow everyone to feel connected and included.

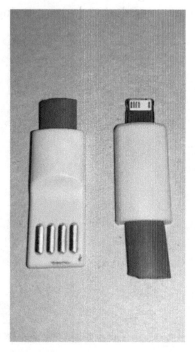

Star Power, adding a little pizzazz and style to anything!

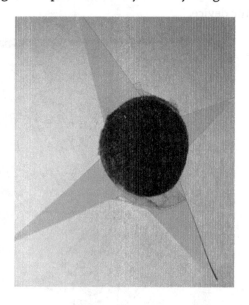

Figure 2, continued

This strap-on energy device provides unlimited energy anytime it's needed.

NAME: _____ DATE: _____

Handout 1.3
Utility Bracelet Superpowers

Directions: Choose two skills or personal qualities you will stow away in your superhero utility bracelet.

Skill or Quality #1:	Skill or Quality #2:
What gadget or tool will represent this quality or skill?	What gadget or tool will represent this quality or skill?

Draw a picture of one of the gadgets or tools above that will serve as a metaphor for your superhero skill or personal quality. You'll need access to this gadget or tool at a moment's notice!

NAME:_____ DATE: _____

Handout 1.3
Utility Bracelet Superpowers Sample

Directions: Choose two skills or personal qualities you will stow away in your superhero utility bracelet.

Skill or Quality #1: *Patience.*	Skill or Quality #2: *Writing and drawing.*
What gadget or tool will represent this quality or skill? *The Patient Bunny is a living gadget. She appears whenever impatience is about to lead to frustration and calms the situation with her cheery, patient presence.*	What gadget or tool will represent this quality or skill? *The sharpest pencil in the world.* *A magical paint brush.* *These weapons are used by the two great and mighty twins, Choco and Sugar Bunny!*

Draw a picture of one of the gadgets or tools above that will serve as a metaphor for your superhero skill or personal quality. You'll need access to this gadget or tool at a moment's notice!

UNIT 1: SUPERHEROES

Lesson 1.4

Engineering Design Challenge

Students are presented with a real-world engineering challenge in this lesson. Can our superheroes draw on their design and engineering skills to meet the requirements for creating a "quick-release" latch for their utility bracelets?

Materials

- » Handout 1.4: Design Challenge Memo
- » Handout 1.4: Latch and Lid Design Rubric
- » Construction paper of various colors
- » Latch and lid materials (use some or all of these):
  - » Paper clips
  - » Pipe cleaners
  - » Beads
  - » Low-temperature hot glue
  - » Duct tape
  - » Other junk drawer items

Estimated Time

- » 30–45 minutes

Procedure

This lesson introduces a real-world design and engineering problem—one of the strongest elements for a STEAM curriculum. The Product Development Department has issued a company memorandum tasking students, who are members of the Superhero Design Team, with designing an effective lid and latch assembly for the superhero utility bracelets. Use Handout 1.4: Design Challenge Memo to launch the design challenge. Distribute latch and lid materials (see Materials).

Here is an opportunity for students to practice strong resilience skills. I've noticed that many of the lid and latch designs are far from effective on first attempts. Encourage students to use creativity and "tinkering" skills to solve this real-world design problem—a true process instead of a "one and done" race to a finished product. You want students to draw upon both skills and a positive mindset to complete a task that might be challenging. You might take the opportunity to speak to persistence and a growth mindset—allowing oneself the grace to be able to fail and try again. A little frustration in a safe classroom atmosphere can be a tremendous opportunity for growth for gifted learners who may have grown accustomed to a fast brand of excellence. Proficiency on this task is simple: Do the lid and the latch work? Is the latch mechanism simple and repeatable? Meeting the challenge, however, is not simple.

Samples are shown in Figure 3, and a one-point rubric appears on Handout 1.4: Latch and Lid Design Rubric.

Figure 3
Sample Utility Bracelets and Latch Designs

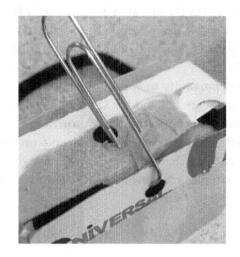

NAME: _____ DATE: _____

Handout 1.4

Design Challenge Memo

Directions: Use the information proved in the following memo to create a lid and latch for your utility bracelet.

Memo: Superhero Design Team
From: Product Development Department

The Lid
» The design of the utility bracelet's lid should allow easy access to the contents.
» When designing the lid, keep in mind that a latch will need to work with it.

The Latch
» Superheroes need a good latch for the utility bracelet. The latch should be easy to use and should work over and over before it needs a repair. A superhero can't be bothered with fixing latches all of the time! Nor can a superhero come to save the day if they are fiddling with a latch that is difficult to open and close.
» Finally, the utility bracelets need to look sharp. Have you ever seen a superhero in a shabby costume? The utility bracelets should be neatly covered with colored paper.
» We superheroes have an image to uphold. Our utility bracelets should make us proud.

NAME: _____ DATE: _____

Handout 1.4

Latch and Lid Design Rubric

Advanced	Proficient	In Progress
	The latch works again and again before needing repair or adjustment.	
	The lid opens easily, and the opening is large enough to remove items.	
	The utility bracelet is covered neatly with solid colored paper.	

Notes:

Lesson 1.5

The Grappling Hook Metaphor

Creating physical metaphors continues in this lesson. This time, students create a grappling hook using materials such as string and paper clips. The grappling hook represents those persons in a student's life whom they can "latch onto" for support.

Materials

- » Handout 1.5: Wonderings: Grappling Hook
- » Handout 1.5: Wonderings: Grappling Hook Sample
- » Materials to create grappling hooks (use some or all of these):
  - » Paper clips
  - » Hot glue
  - » Scrap wood pieces
  - » String

Estimated Time

- » 30–45 minutes

Procedure

Tell students: *Everyone—even superheroes—needs someone they can rely on, share their thoughts and dreams with, laugh alongside, and hold onto when needed. We all need a "grappling hook." This is why we will all add a grappling hook to our superhero utility bracelets.*

To demonstrate how a grappling hook works, share this amusing compilation from *Gravity Falls*: https://www.youtube.com/watch?v=ADrmDqKrAfQ. Explain: *Aside from the*

Figure 4
Grappling Hook Example

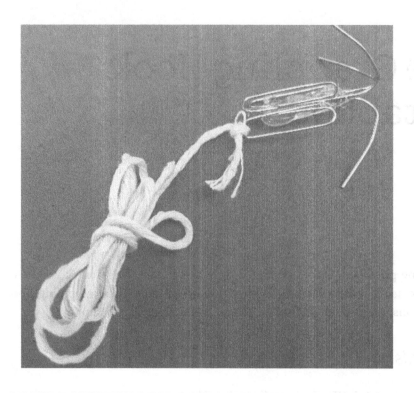

amusing, almost superhero-ish, cartoon, let's take note of the qualities of a grappling hook and how they might be helpful. Complete the graphic organizer about grappling hooks.

Have students break down the grappling hook metaphor using the graphic organizer on Handout 1.5: Wonderings: Grappling Hook, which encourages them to cite the "grappling hooks" in their lives. Sample answers are provided on the page following the handout.

After this groundwork is laid, challenge each student to create a grappling hook to remind them of those people most dear to them. Any materials on hand may be used. My students have made mini grappling hooks from paper clips, hot glue, scrap wood pieces, and string. Figure 4 shows one of these creations. Once students have finished, they can add the miniature grappling hooks to their utility bracelets (where there is room).

NAME:_____ DATE: _____

Handout 1.5
Wonderings: Grappling Hook

Directions: How can a grappling hook be more than itself? Consider the following questions to begin your wonderings.

Describe a grappling hook in words or pictures.

How is it used? What is its purpose?

UNIT 1: SUPERHEROES

NAME: _____ DATE: _____

Handout 1.5: Wonderings: Grappling Hook, *continued*

How do people feel about it?

What connections can you make between a grappling hook and your own life?

I'm beginning to think this thing is more than it seems . . . _____
_____
_____
_____

NAME:_____ DATE: _____

Handout 1.5

Wonderings: Grappling Hook Sample

Directions: How can a grappling hook be more than itself? Consider the following questions to begin your wonderings.

Describe a grappling hook in words or pictures.

It is used to reach things that cannot be reached easily. A grappling hook lifts you up when you hold onto it. It's a tool that can help you do amazing things or get you out of a tough situation.

How is it used? What is its purpose?

It is made of metal, has hooks and arms, and is attached to a cord or rope. It can be thrown or launched.

NAME: _____ DATE: _____

Handout 1.5: Wonderings: Grappling Hook Sample, *continued*

How do people feel about it?

I have never used a real one, but I have seen them in action movies. I would like to try one out by climbing onto the roof of my house when Dad is up there making repairs. That would be really funny when he turned around and saw me smiling at him and twirling the hook around in my hand.

What connections can you make between a grappling hook and your own life?

Grappling hooks are ways to get out of trouble, reach safety, or reach places we couldn't get to without them. They could be seen as anything or any person that supports us and makes us feel safer and more confident.

I'm beginning to think a circle is more than it seems . . . *Grappling hooks are ways to get out of trouble, reach safety, or reach places we couldn't get to without them. They could be seen as anything or any person that supports us and makes us feel safer and more confident.*

Lesson 1.6

Perfectionism Shield

In this lesson students will make a "shield" against perfectionistic thoughts by creating a symbol to stand for each thought. As Pyryt (2004) stated, "There is a fine line between striving to reach high standards of excellence and feeling self-defeated through the inability to reach unrealistic expectations of perfection" (p. 11). All too often, we see our gifted learners fall into this trap.

For more information about the relationship between gifted learners and perfectionism, see my articles from the NAGC Blog, "Surfing a Wave of Wonderfulness" (https://www.nagc.org/blog/surfing-wave-wonderfulness) or "Growing Up Generation Z and Gifted: Bomb Cyclone Perfectionism" (https://nagc.org/blog/growing-generation-z-and-gifted-bomb-cyclone-perfectionism). These articles are written for both parents and teachers of gifted learners.

Materials

- » Handout 1.6: Perfectionism Shield
- » Handout 1.6: Perfectionism Shield Sample
- » Paper plates (one per student)
- » Pens, markers, and colored pencils

Estimated Time

- » 50 minutes

Procedure

Discuss Perfectionism. Discuss and review perfectionism with students, perhaps sharing the quote from Pyryt (2004): "There is a fine line between striving to reach high standards of excellence and feeling self-defeated through the inability to reach unrealistic expectations of perfection" (p. 11). Tell students: *Superheroes face the same challenges! When everything so often comes easily, how disabling it must be when a challenge comes along which is not easily met.*

Create Symbols. As a class, discuss and clarify the perfectionist thoughts on Handout 1.6: Perfectionism Shield and provide additional examples of each type of thought. Then, have students create a symbol for each of the three perfectionist thoughts. Students may create their own symbols individually, or the class may create them together.

Creating metaphors is a complex task, and my students have experienced varying degrees of success. Most kids struggled to some degree to create good metaphors for the shields. Several cartooned the ideas instead of creating metaphors—that's acceptable, as we want to challenge them to extend their abilities appropriately. In addition to Handout 1.6: Perfectionism Shield Sample, see Figure 5 for examples of symbols. The three clustered images build on the idea of the "shadows of failure."

Create Shields. Decorated paper plates make excellent mini-shields to guard against unhealthy perfectionism. Distribute paper plates to students and explain how they will create their shields. Students will transform the symbols they've created on Handout 1.6: Perfectionism Shield in order to design the shield—adding color and details to make the shields stand out boldly.

Willing students in my classroom hung their shields outside my classroom door. I chose to add a sign that read, "You're Safe Here," to our display. I always hope my classroom is a safe place for all students to display their talents in a spirit of camaraderie and acceptance. Figure 6 features one of the finished shields from one of my classes. This student used ninjas to represent three perfectionistic thoughts.

Figure 5
Perfectionism Symbol Examples

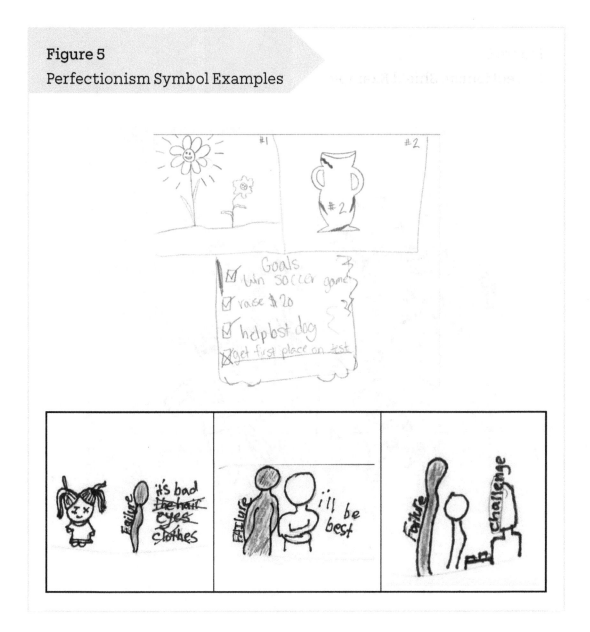

Figure 6
Perfectionism Shield Example

NAME: _____ DATE: _____

Handout 1.6

Perfectionism Shield

Directions: Write an example of each of the perfectionist thoughts below. Then, create a symbol for each thought.

Thought #1: All-or-Nothing "If it's not perfect, then it must be worthless."	Thought #2: Wants Become Demands "I don't just want something good to happen; it *must* happen!"	Thought #3: Focusing on Unmet Goals Instead of Success "I must be a failure because I haven't met *all* of my goals."
Example:	Example:	Example:
Symbol:	Symbol:	Symbol:

Social and Emotional Curriculum for Gifted Students, Grade 4 © Prufrock Press Inc.

NAME: _____ DATE: _____

Handout 1.6
Perfectionism Shield Sample

Directions: Write an example of each of the perfectionist thoughts below. Then, create a symbol for each thought.

Thought #1: All-or-Nothing	Thought #2: Wants Become Demands	Thought #3: Focusing on Unmet Goals Instead of Success
"If it's not perfect, then it must be worthless."	"I don't just want something good to happen; it *must* happen!"	"I must be a failure because I haven't met *all* of my goals."
Example: *A student starts to cry because she finds a couple of errors in an amazing project. She thinks she has ruined it.*	Example: *A student starts off by wanting to be one of the highest scorers on his soccer team but starts believing he must be the top scorer.*	Example: *A student reaches the extra-challenge level of online math but can't stop worrying about the bonus level left incomplete.*
Symbol: Restaur⊗nt	Symbol: 	Symbol: 4+3x(5+8)= ?

UNIT 1: SUPERHEROES

38   *Social and Emotional Curriculum for Gifted Students, Grade 4* © Prufrock Press Inc.

Lesson 1.7

Sidekicks

For Lesson 1.7, students will create a superhero sidekick—a companion to support them on their daily path as they navigate social and emotional challenges.

Materials

- » Handout 1.7: Meet the Sidekick
- » Handout 1.7: Meet the Sidekick Sample
- » Wooden clothespins, paint sticks, or paper doll cutouts (one per student)

Estimated Time

- » 60 minutes

Procedure

Discuss and Plan Sidekicks. Tell students: *Every superhero could use a good sidekick. Sidekicks often lend lighthearted relief to situations as well as provide support. Not all sidekicks are made the same.* Share and discuss the following statements about sidekicks:
- » Some sidekicks react to the overreactions and overreaches of heroes.
- » Some sidekicks take a superhero's good qualities and exaggerate them in a ridiculous way.
- » Some sidekicks take a superhero's bad qualities and exaggerate them in a ridiculous way.
- » Some sidekicks make up for gaps in a hero's abilities.
- » Some sidekicks come to the rescue.

- » Some sidekicks complement a hero's abilities.
- » Some sidekicks do a little bit of all of these things.

Ask students to provide examples from sidekicks they know about in the superhero world.

Tell students that they will plan a sidekick using Handout 1.7: Meet the Sidekick, which asks them to decide the name, characteristics, and appearance of their sidekick. Handout 1.7: Meet the Sidekick Sample shares an example of a sidekick, Derpy Dog, whose positive qualities are dependability, writing, and a friendly attitude.

Build Sidekicks. Once students have completed their planning sheets, they will work to "build" their sidekick from the materials you have provided. Large wooden clothespins are fun to use to make sidekicks. Paint sticks also work well and might even be donated by your local hardware store. Examples of completed sidekicks, including Derpy Dog, may be found in Figure 7. There you will also see Sky Skittlemaker—always positive and adding brilliant colors to her superhero's life. Her rainbow booster spreads happy rainbows into our world, reminding us to stay positive and look on the bright side.

Follow-Up: Bonus Activities

Other activities that might build upon this unit include:
- » Create a comic strip adventure about your superhero.
- » Design a logo for your superhero.
- » Design a helmet for your superhero.
- » Design a costume for your superhero.

See Figure 8 for an example of a hero's helmet. The pencil helmet helps everyone feel at home, accepted, and valued. The pencils shoot out phrases, including compliments, encouragement, and warm greetings. Feeling different? Feeling alienated? This pencil-helmeted superhero is a connector at heart, helping all of those around feel comforted.

Unit 1: Superheroes

Figure 7
Clothespin Sidekicks

Figure 8
Hero's Helmet Example

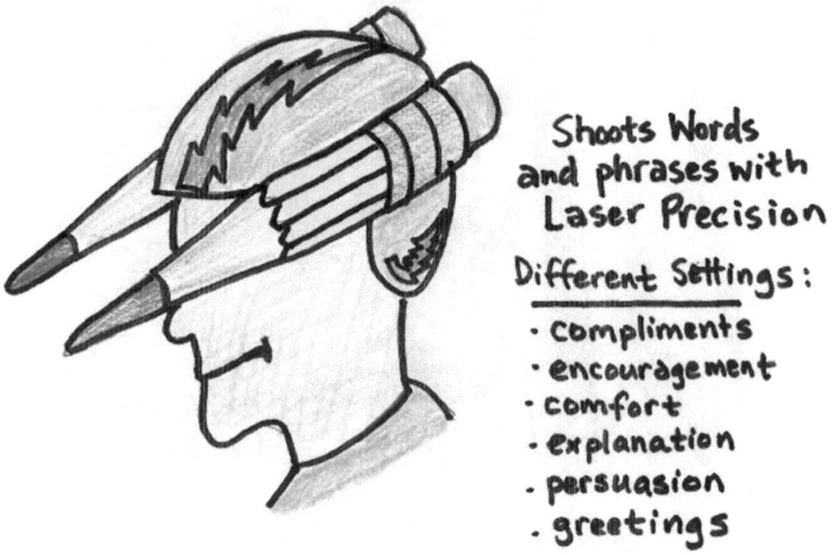

Shoots words and phrases with Laser Precision

Different Settings:
- compliments
- encouragement
- comfort
- explanation
- persuasion
- greetings

NAME: _____ DATE: _____

Handout 1.7

Meet the Sidekick

Directions: Use this planning sheet to decide the name and characteristics of your sidekick. Decorate the silhouette with your sidekick's physical features and costume.

Sidekick's name:

Overheard saying to our hero:

Item or costume choice special to the sidekick:

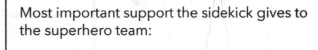

Most important support the sidekick gives to the superhero team:

Social and Emotional Curriculum for Gifted Students, Grade 4 © Prufrock Press Inc.

UNIT 1: SUPERHEROES

43

NAME:_____ DATE:_____

Handout 1.7

Meet the Sidekick Sample

Directions: Use this planning sheet to decide the name and characteristics of your sidekick. Decorate the silhouette with your sidekick's physical features and costume.

Sidekick's name: *Derpy Dog*

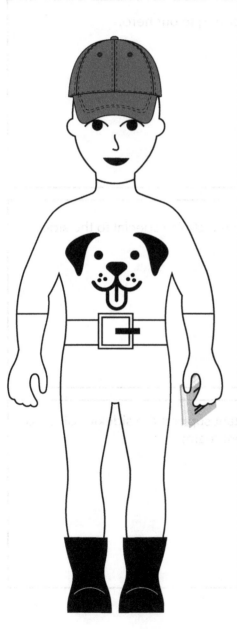

Overheard saying to our hero:

"Do you always have to follow the rules all of the time? Have some fun!"

Item or costume choice special to the sidekick:

Pocket illustration pad to add color and dazzle to the writer's stories.

Most important support the sidekick gives to the superhero team:

When our hero starts taking life too seriously and worrying about everything in the world, the sidekick steps in with a good joke or a funny cartoon drawing to remind our hero to have a little fun. Derpy Dog is also the best shortstop in the school and does a hilarious impression of Derpy Dracula.

UNIT 2

Spy Training
Self-Esteem

Background

Are your students a little reluctant to engage in social-emotional discussions? In this unit, students use their imaginations and have a blast while addressing affective gifted and talented standards. Your kids will be enthusiastic participants in a spy training academy while sorting through key ideas in the social-emotional realm. Sound a little far-fetched? Well, this *is* top secret stuff. Some of it may be amazing.

Our would-be spies must undergo psychological training in order to understand others and themselves, including their own strengths and limitations. Students read a case study of a student who thinks he is heaven's gift on Earth, analyze this student's behavior, and role-play advice they might give. This fictional student must have unrealistic self-esteem, but what is unrealistic self-esteem, anyway? Spies better learn about realistic and respectful self-esteem while they are in training.

With an understanding of self-esteem in hand, it's time for students to go on a training mission—helping themselves and a friend with an affirmation. Students write these affirmations and deliver them in a stealthy manner befitting a spy: writing notes on tiny slips of paper, tucking them inside gel caps, and leaving secret instructions for others to find the gel caps in a dead drop inside the school.

What legacy would a person want to leave? How will they want to be remembered? What would they like others to say about them? When students have learned about respectful and realistic self-esteem, they can easily imagine a positive legacy. Working from legacies, our students—spies in training—must imagine a legend for themselves. As undercover agents, they'll have to create a fake identity or legend. Why not use this legend to imagine the ways their talents and abilities might take them into an exciting career in the future? Students will set about creating a case file for their legendary selves, complete with items confiscated from their pockets (metaphors for their good qualities), a future certificate of achievement, and a page torn from their "hopes and dreams" diary.

Unit Objectives

Students will:
- » affirm realistic and respectful self-esteem, and
- » form a vision of their future success.

NAGC Learning and Development Standards

1.1. Self-Understanding. Students with gifts and talents demonstrate self-knowledge with respect to their interests, strengths, identities, and needs in socio-emotional development and in intellectual, academic, creative, leadership, and artistic domains.

1.3. Self-Understanding. Students with gifts and talents demonstrate understanding of and respect for similarities and differences between themselves and their peer group and others in the general population.

1.6. Cognitive and Affective Growth. Students with gifts and talents benefit from meaningful and challenging learning activities addressing their unique characteristics and needs.

1.8. Cognitive and Affective Growth. Students with gifts and talents identify future career goals that match their talents and abilities and resources needed to meet those goals (e.g., higher education opportunities, mentors, financial support).

Themes and Skills Addressed

Social-Emotional Themes
- » Friendship
- » Goal setting
- » Growth mindset
- » Humility
- » Gratitude
- » Multipotentiality
- » Identity
- » Social problem solving
- » Psychosocial development

Academic Skills
- » Role-playing
- » Metaphor creation
- » Graphic design
- » Building and engineering

Launch

The first task in this unit is to help students understand themselves and others better. Ask students the following question and discuss as a class: *Why do spies need to have a good understanding of themselves and others?*

Some answers to discuss include:

- » We must know our limitations and strengths in a realistic way in order to carry out missions. If we think we can accomplish anything, then we could be in for a rude awakening!
- » We must be able to anticipate the actions of others—to get inside their minds and understand what they might be thinking—so that we may plan carefully and react quickly.

Lesson 2.1

Understanding Self-Esteem

This lesson about self-esteem incorporates role-play, an excellent way to practice social situations. In the process of role-playing, students process real-life situations, generate solutions, and meet conflict in a nonthreatening way. By playing a role, students remove personal doubts and fears. It's much easier to solve social problems when pretending to be someone else. Additionally, creative dramatics:

> stimulates thinking, problem solving, and imagination, while encouraging awareness and concentration, helps develop emotional self-control, strengthens self-confidence in speaking and performing, develops individuality, enhances knowledge and understanding, provides insight, relies on key content, and provides opportunity for informal formative assessment of student knowledge. (Sumners & Hines, 2020, p. 7)

Materials

- » Handout 2.1: The Story of Student A
- » Handout 2.1: Self-Esteem
- » Handout 2.1: Realistic and Respectful Statements
- » Handout 2.1: Role-Play Challenge
- » Handout 2.1: My Legacy

Estimated Time

- » 60 minutes

Procedure

Share the following activities with students. You may either project the handouts onto a screen, distribute them as activity sheets, or share them orally. These activities are not intended as "sit and get" but need to be shared and discussed. Also, they are not just worksheets or writing assignments. You might choose to ask students to jot down answers here or there, but that is totally up to you. These activities are meant to spur thinking and generate discussion.

Activity 1: Student A. Share Handout 2.1: The Story of Student A and read about Student A's experiences. Answer the questions together as a class, and have fun with the role-play challenge.

Key points for discussion include:
» Student A wants attention and wants everyone to think he is brilliant.
» Instead, he annoys everyone and is probably on his way to losing friends if he hasn't lost them already.

As with any social situation, there are is no fool-proof advice or answers as to how Student A might adjust his behaviors to create a more positive response from his teacher and classmates. Gifted learners, however, are full of insight and understanding and are able to understand another's perspective at a young age. After students have unpacked their analysis, they'll try out real-world responses in the role-playing activity. Here is an opportunity to practice a social situation in which they tactfully advise Student A.

Activity 2: Self-Esteem Definition. Share the definition of self-esteem on Handout 2.1: Self-Esteem. Lead student discussions toward a focus on *realistic* and *respectful* self-esteem (Galbraith, 2009, p. 65). This activity refers back to and extends the previous activity about Student A.

Key points for discussion include:
» By being honest with ourselves about our abilities and areas in which we need to improve, we respect ourselves.
» By being realistic, we don't brag. Nor are we hard on ourselves for not being perfect.
» Self-esteem means *respecting yourself* for what you can do and *challenging yourself* to improve at the same time.

Follow-up by sharing Handout 2.1: Realistic and Respectful Statements. Have students circle the statements that are realistic and/or respectful. Then, reach a consensus together as a class.

Activity 3: Role-Play. Use the activity prompt on Handout 2.1: Role-Play Challenge to role-play bragging, realistic, and unfair statements of self-esteem. Students can work with a partner or in groups of three. Groups should choose one role-playing response to share with the class. Make it clear that practiced performances are not expected and that role-playing is improvised. Let's not get bogged down with rehearsals and scripts here.

Activity 4: Legacies. For what actions, attitudes, accomplishments, and kindnesses does a person want to be known? Have students complete Handout 2.1: My Legacy as a way to support self-esteem. Hold on to their completed legacy statements. Students will need them later in this unit when creating their case files.

NAME:_____ DATE: _____

Handout 2.1

The Story of Student A

Directions: Consider the story about Student A. Then reflect on the questions that follow.

During math time, Mrs. Stevens challenged the class with a math brain teaser. The students' faces were full of looks of confusion as they put pencil to paper and tried to solve the problem. One student—we will just call him *Student A*—did not have a confused look on his face.

Student A looked up, smiling to see if anyone else noticed. They did not. He beamed. He shuffled his paper. Still, no one looked at him. Student A made a big scratching sound on his paper as he wrote and circled the answer to the brain teaser. Then, he announced loudly, "Done!"

He waved the paper over his head, his voice booming, "Mrs. Stevens, what do we do with these when we are done? That was easy! What do I do while I'm waiting for everyone else to finish?"

Later, when the class broke into groups, students excitedly joined groups of threes, fours, or fives. Students looking for a group quickly found others to join . . . everyone except Student A, who sat alone at his desk without a group. Nobody invited Student A to join them.

1. What are your thoughts and impressions after reading this story?

2. How would you describe Student A? Support your opinion with details from the story.

3. How would you feel if you were one of Student A's classmates?

NAME:_____ DATE: _____

Handout 2.1: The Story of Student A, *continued*

4. Why does no one ask Student A to join their group?

5. What advice, if any, would you give Student A?

Challenge

With a partner, role-play advice you might give to Student A. How do you imagine Student A might react? Will it make a difference how the advice is given and what is said?

NAME:_____ DATE: _____

Handout 2.1
Self-Esteem

Directions: Consider the following definition of *self-esteem* and answer the questions that follow.

Self-esteem is the respect you have for:
- » yourself,
- » your skills and talents,
- » your beliefs and attitudes, and
- » your abilities.

According to Judy Galbraith in *The Gifted Kids' Survival Guide*, "Self-esteem doesn't mean bragging or exaggerating about who you are and what you can do. It means being realistic–honest–about who you are, inside and out. That includes knowing your strengths and knowing what you need to work on."

1. What does the definition of self-esteem mean to you? Put it in your own words.

2. Why is respecting oneself a part of the definition?

3. Are skills and talents two different things? Are skills and talents different from abilities?

NAME:_____ DATE: _____

Handout 2.1: Self-Esteem, *continued*

4. What is the difference between bragging and honest self-esteem?

5. Why is knowing what you need to improve upon part of self-esteem?

6. Why is being honest with yourself an important part of self-esteem?

7. How does a person act when they respect themselves?

8. Does Student A have healthy self-esteem? Why would he act the way he does?

NAME:_____ DATE: _____

Handout 2.1
Realistic and Respectful Statements

Directions: Circle the statements that are realistic and respectful.

I enjoy learning.

I'm lucky that I can do a lot of different things.

I almost always win.

I'm terrible.

I like a challenge.

That's so easy!

I can always improve.

I expect to try hard and to do well.

No way can I do that!

Only us smart kids get to be in gifted and talented classes.

Everyone is unique with different strengths.

NAME:_____ DATE: _____

Handout 2.1
Role-Play Challenge

Directions: Working with a partner or in a group of three, act out three different self-esteem responses for a situation in which a person is nervous about a challenge they are facing (e.g., performing a solo performance for the school). See the example role-play below for how this might look. Then, consider the planning questions as you create your role-play.

Example

Challenging situation: A person is about to sing a solo in a school performance.

First, a person walks in, strikes a pose with a huge smile, tilts their head back, and announces, "I hope everyone doesn't feel bad when I get the biggest applause. My mom says I'm a natural talent. I can't help it!" (This person displays bragging/unhealthy self-esteem.)

Second, a person walks in with a smile, saying, "I'm a little nervous, but I think we will do great tonight! We have all practiced hard, and we're going to give it our best!" (This person displays healthy self-esteem.)

Third, a person walks in and slumps into a chair, saying, "I bet nobody is going to like me. They will know my voice is bad. If they clap, it's because they feel sorry for me." (This person displays unfair and perfectionistic behavior.)

Planning Questions

Consider these questions as you create your role-play:
1. What will the challenging situation be, and how will you act it?
2. In this situation, what will a person who is bragging and not showing healthy self-esteem say? How will these words be spoken?
3. What will a person who is showing healthy self-esteem say? How will these words be spoken?
4. What will a person who is unfair to themselves, unhealthy, and perfectionistic say? How will these words be spoken?

Notes or Storyboard

NAME:_____   DATE:_____

Handout 2.1
My Legacy

Directions: One definition of *legacy* is the life story we leave behind. A legacy is something for which we are known and remembered. We build our legacies every day by the way we treat others, the decisions we make, the skills and talents we develop, and the hard work of living our dreams.

What legacy would you like to leave? What legacy would you like to be known for? In the box below, write what you would like others to say about you—now and in the future. Make sure what is said is positive, realistic, respectful, and fair.

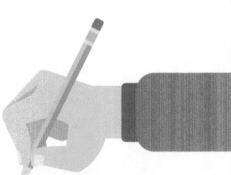

Social and Emotional Curriculum for Gifted Students, Grade 4 © Prufrock Press Inc.

Lesson 2.2

Internalizing Positive Self-Esteem: Dead Drops

Now students are ready to put their self-esteem spy training to the test. In this lesson, students will write two secret messages and store them inside the gel caps. Yes, a spy may have to eat evidence or secret messages! This is why I suggest providing size 0 gelatin caps for this lesson. Important: *Students will not actually consume these gel caps* (although one of my students did eat one once, and I am happy to report he survived it).

This lesson also contains instructions for students to complete the "dead drops" of their messages. You might give them these instructions in some secret, spy-worthy way. One fun way, for example, is the old "20 questions" game in which spies must use their powers of deduction. Hide the papers somewhere in the classroom and have students ask 20 questions to find them. Students may not get up from their seats and must ask only "yes" or "no" questions to locate the papers.

Materials

- » Handout 2.2: Super Booster Advertisement
- » Handout 2.2: Spy Training Mission
- » Empty 0 size gel caps (two per student)
- » Paper and scissors

Estimated Time

- » 30 minutes

Procedure

Internalizing Positive Self-Esteem. This opening activity will remind students about what they've learned concerning positive, realistic, and respectful self-esteem. It will also serve as a transition to the positive messages students will create in the dead drop activity. Share the advertisement shown in Handout 2.2: Super Booster Advertisement. In a whole-class discussion, have students consider the following questions:
- » How is the advertisement accurate?
- » What would you add to it?
- » What does it mean to "internalize" these ideas?

Dead Drops. In this lesson, students will write two secret messages and store them inside gel caps. One message will be an affirmation given to them by another student spy. The other message will be a self-directed "secret mission" goal in life. Tell students: *Both of these are important messages that we need to internalize. We're using the gel caps to represent internalizing or swallowing the message. Remember: We will not actually eat these pills!*

Have your student spies work on writing and placing messages in two gel caps.

One gel cap should contain a reminder about the student's own chosen legacy. Students will place these inside their desks or cubbies and store them away for safekeeping.

A second gel cap should be a written affirmation for another person inside the school (see the frequently asked questions in Tips and Instructions for Dead Drops for possible recipients). These messages will be short, specific notes to boost positive feelings in another person. For example, "I like the way you smile nearly every day when you come into class" is much more specific than "You are happy, and I like that." Likewise, "You always try to include others. I've seen you invite others to play with us on the playground many times" is much more specific than "You are a good friend." Writing messages in tiny letters on tiny strips of paper is a fun challenge for students. Even rolling up the tiny message so it will fit inside a gel cap brings smiles. The second gel cap, the affirmation written for another person in the school, should be delivered as a dead drop:

> Dead drop: (n) When one spy leaves an inconspicuous-looking item in a particular location for a colleague to pick up later. A notorious dead drop location is a trash can. One spy might simply look as if they are throwing away old fast food wrappers when, inside, a secret message is written. They'd better not wait too long, though. The custodian might come along and empty the trash!

The following dead drop rules are also contained in the student directions on Handout 2.2: Spy Training Mission:
- » The dead drop must be in a location inside the school.
- » In order for the mission to be successful, the gel cap must be found only by the intended recipient.
- » The teacher will not mention anything about the dead drops. However, if any gel caps are noticed and a student says something like, "Hey, what is this pill doing here?" then the mission will be deemed unsuccessful.

- » The goal is for 100% of the missions to be successful.
- » Each spy has one week to complete the mission.

Remind students of this important note: *Do not actually swallow these gel caps! Internalizing this message is a metaphor—or symbolic. Let's discuss what this means as a class.*

Tips and Instructions for Dead Drops

- » While conducting this activity, I sent an email to the school staff explaining what my students were doing. I asked staff members to allow students to hide the messages in their classrooms. If a message was hidden in a teacher's classroom, then the teacher promised to help keep the secret.
- » The email also said that if any staff member found a message in the school outside of their room, then they should bring the message to me as a failed mission.
- » Any messages left in my room were "off-limits" to other spies (I had three different groups hiding messages at one time) but could be found by non-spies (all my other groups not doing the spy unit). Most messages were hidden around the school somewhere or in another teacher's classroom and not in my room.
- » Some examples of hiding places: the gym, hallways, nooks and crannies, the milk cooler in the lunchroom, a coat rack, and the lost and found (how ironic).
- » Frequently asked questions:
  - » May the messages be hidden at home? *No. Too easy.*
  - » Can messages be delivered to a brother or sister? *Yes. As long as the brother or sister attends the school.*
  - » Can a message be delivered to a teacher? *Yes.*
  - » Can a message be delivered to a student in another grade? *Yes.*
  - » Can a message be delivered to another spy? *Yes, but maybe that's too easy . . . so it's not recommended.*
  - » How do I tell the other person about where to find my message? *You figure it out—but you'd better be sneaky!*

Dead Drop Example. Students can get quite creative with these dead drops. One of my students placed his dead drop inside a pink mitten in the lost and found. He assumed that because the mitten had no partner, it probably would not be claimed. He used a "rubber band secret message" to deliver the first clue to his recipient. In this method, a rubber band is stretched out tightly (putting the rubber band around a coffee can works well for this), and a message is written on the rubber band while it is stretched. When the rubber band is relaxed, the message shows up illegibly tiny. The rubber band has to be stretched out again in order for the message to be read. The added bonus to rubber band messages is in the delivery—boing!—as it can be shot toward its recipient. (*Note.* I warned the student's classroom teacher that he was going to be shooting a rubber band across the classroom.) The student's first message said, "I have an important message for you. Find me feeling pink and lost. Ask Mrs.

Foster." The student had talked to two different teachers to help deliver his dead drop clues. The first teacher, Mrs. Foster, was asked to deliver the next message to the recipient, which was "My hand is going to get really cold with just one mitten! Talk to the recess teacher." The recess teacher, Mrs. Isreal, said to the recipient, "I am forever picking up lost mittens out here and putting them in the lost and found." Message delivered. The affirmation in the capsule read, "Something I admire: You keep trying even when things are the most difficult."

My students loved the dead drop activity. I received enthusiastic reports throughout the week. About 90% of the 35 missions were successful in the end.

NAME:_____ DATE: _____

Handout 2.2

Super Booster Advertisement

SUPER BOOSTER

Energy all day, EVERY DAY!

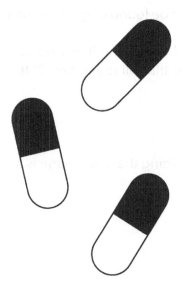

Positive
Realistic
Respectful
Fair

THE #1 WAY TO INTERNALIZE SELF-ESTEEM

UNIT 2: SPY TRAINING

NAME:_____   DATE: _____

Handout 2.2

Spy Training Mission

Directions: Write an affirmation for another student or teacher. Deliver the affirmation inside a gel cap in a dead drop. Your teacher will answer further questions and will supply further instructions.

> Dead drop: (n) When one spy leaves an inconspicuous-looking item in a particular location for a colleague to pick up later. A notorious dead drop location is a trash can. One spy might simply look as if they are throwing away old fast food wrappers when, inside, a secret message is written. But they'd better not wait too long—the custodian might come along and empty the trash!

Dead Drop Rules
- The dead drop must be in a location inside the school.
- In order for the mission to be successful, the gel cap must be found only by the intended recipient.
- Your teacher will not mention anything about the dead drops, but if any gel caps are noticed and a student says something like, "Hey, what is this pill doing here?" then the mission will be deemed unsuccessful.
- Our goal is to have 100% of the missions successful.
- Each spy has one week to complete the mission.

Important note: Do not actually swallow these gel caps! Internalizing these message is a metaphor—or symbolic.

Lesson 2.3

Creating a Legend and Case File

A mix between imaginative fun and serious thought about future goals, this lesson is about imagining success, dreaming about "someday," seeing oneself successful in life, and finding one's way.

Materials

- » Handout 2.3: Your Case File and Legend
- » Handout 2.3: Case File Data Sheet
- » Handout 2.3: Case File Data Sheet Sample
- » File folders (one per student; may be recycled from previous use)

Estimated Time

- » 20 minutes

Procedure

Invite students to think about their talents and how they might use them someday. What career can they imagine themselves a part of in the future? What expertise and skill do they have to offer the world? This career will help them create their spy cover identities and legends.

Undercover spies may need to create a cover identity or legend. Explain these concepts:
- » A cover identity is a fake identity that a spy takes on to protect their real identity and their real missions.
- » A legend is the story behind the cover identity. Spies must know their legends absolutely forward and backward: Where were you born? Who are you parents? What

Social and Emotional Curriculum for Gifted Students Grade 4

school did you go to? Have you ever broken a bone? Who is your favorite player on your favorite pro football team from your fake hometown? One slip-up could be a disaster!

Have students look over the directions on Handout 2.3: Your Case File and Legend to begin thinking about their legends and creating their case files. Distribute file folders for students to label and decorate. In this portion of the lesson, students create their own legends by imagining what their lives will be like in the future once they have fulfilled their legacies—their hopes and dreams.

Then, distribute Handout 2.3: Case File Data Sheet and have students complete the information about their secret identities. I have found that these work well as a self-paced set of activities. Some students are very quick and can easily move from activity to activity. A sample data sheet is included on the page following the handout.

NAME: _____   DATE: _____

Handout 2.3
Your Case File and Legend

Directions: We're going to go in depth into your "fake" life through a creative case file project. Undercover agents create cover identities and legends. As an undercover agent, you will need to know your legend inside and out, or you risk being exposed.

You will create your legend, your cover identity, based on how you see yourself living out your legacy in the future: How will you achieve your hopes and dreams? What accomplishments will you have completed? What career will you have chosen? What difference will you make in the world?

Any goal begins with thinking, dreaming, wishing, and hoping. Be creative. Think positively. You have wonderful abilities. How will you use them someday? Let's build this legacy by imagining our future selves fulfilling our dreams!

Case File

Begin building your legend with a case file. Even though this task is top secret, you will need to share information with your teacher and will want to share ideas with fellow spies-in-training. You will use a file folder for your case file. Label the folder with your legend name, and add the words "Top Secret" or "Classified" to the front. Is it an FBI or CIA file? You may want to add that label as well. Inside your case file, you will place your Case File Data Sheet.

NAME: _____ DATE: _____

Handout 2.3

Case File Data Sheet

Directions: Complete the data sheet with information about your legend. Directions for completing each step are included on the following page.

Surveillance Photo

Name: _____

Also Known as: _____

_____

_____

_____

Born: _____ Place: _____

Known Residence: _____

Identifying Characteristics: 1. _____

2. _____

3. _____

Known Associates: _____

_____

Career: _____

NAME:_____ DATE: _____

Handout 2.3: Case File Data Sheet, *continued*

Completing the Data Sheet:
- **Also Known As:** Create a name that is common and does not stand out. Some students use names from favorite book characters (a unique combination of different names—you wouldn't want to be named Harry Potter), sports stars, or parts of their middle names. Don't choose a name that makes you look suspicious!
- **Surveillance Photo:** Oh, dang! You are now a suspected spy. Another spy snapped a surveillance photo of you while you happened to be doing the hard work of making your legacy hopes and dreams come true. What hard work were you doing? Draw the picture in the rectangle on the left, and write a caption for the picture on the right.
- **Born:** In what year is your undercover identity's birth? You'd better make it fit with how old you look right now. Most students change the month and day but keep the actual year they were born. Also, where were you born? Make it a place you are familiar with but not where you were actually born. Supplying accurate details about this place will make your cover look more legitimate.
- **Known Residence:** Where will you live in the future? You may have to live in a specific location to make your legend real. For example, if you would like to be a wildlife photographer, then you may have to live near a city and airport to make it easier for you to travel to locations around the world.
- **Identifying Characteristics:** Write three personality traits related to your legacy. How will you act? What important qualities do you have inside of you? What important traits of your personality will allow you to achieve greatness or notoriety? What behaviors will you be known for (not achievements, but behaviors)?
- **Known Associates:** Who was, is, or will be an important, supportive person in your life? Who will be an important person or persons to help you make your goals come true? Name as many people as you can think of.

NAME:_____ DATE: _____

Handout 2.3

Case File Data Sheet Sample

Directions: Complete the data sheet with information about your legend.

Name: *Nicholas Davis*

Also Known as: *Steven Jackson*

Late at night in a laboratory, Steven Jackson seeks a cure for cancer.

Born: *2/20/2007*   Place: *Denver, CO*

Known Residence: *Palo Alto, CA*

Identifying Characteristics: 1. *Tired, baggy eyes*

　　　　　　　　　　　　　　　2. *Laptop under arm*

　　　　　　　　　　　　　　　3. *Notepage, chewed-up pencil*

Known Associates: *Father, mother, sister, Jonas Salk*

Career: *Surgeon and research scientist in medical field*

Lesson 2.4

What's in Your Pockets?

In Lesson 2.4, students create physical metaphors for their most important personality characteristic, their thoughts, and their vision of future success.

Materials

- » Handout 2.4: What's in Your Pockets?
- » Handout 2.4: What's in Your Pockets? Sample
- » Quart-sized plastic bags to collect "evidence" (one per student)
- » Craft materials to create items (e.g., cardstock, cardboard, construction paper, paper clips, pipe cleaners, beads, thin foam sheets or felt, markers, colored pencils, yarn, etc.)

Estimated Time

- » 60 minutes

Procedure

Identify Pocket Items. Tell students: *You'd better be careful! As a suspected spy, you have been brought in for questioning and have been asked to empty your pockets. What evidence would be found in them? This evidence needs to fit your legacy and legend. Make sure your cover identity matches the contents of your pockets. Anything out of place may send you to prison—or worse!*

Explain further: *What items would be found in your future self's pockets? These items metaphorically represent your thoughts, achievements, and personality.* Share Handout 2.4: What's in Your Pockets? and review the directions. Students will identify three items that might be found in their pockets. One item will represent a general personality characteristic, another will represent their thoughts, and a third item will represent their most important future achievement. Share Handout 2.4: What's in Your Pockets? Sample, which follows Steven Jackson's medical science legend.

Create Pocket Items. After students have completed the handout with their metaphorical items, tell them that they will participate in a fun 3-D art project by creating the items and dropping them into an evidence bag to be included with the case file.

Distribute quart-size plastic bags and craft materials. Figure 9 shows Steven Jackson's three metaphorical items: a bandage representing healing and protecting others by finding a cure to cancer, a safety pin that shows he wants to be helpful and kind, and an ant (because ants never give up—just like him).

Students should add their completed items to the case file in an evidence bag.

Unit 2: Spy Training

Figure 9
Evidence Item Examples

71

NAME: _____ DATE: _____

Handout 2.4

What's in Your Pockets?

Directions: Complete the flowchart to help create your legend.

Name (Fake Identity Name): _____					
What is an important personality characteristic you have?	→	How do you know? Give an example.	→	Case File Item 1	
What is an important thought you often think—a thought that helps others know who you are?	→	What does this thought say about you?	→	Case File Item 2	
What will someday be your most important achievement?	→	How is this achievement related to your legacy?	→	Case File Item 3	

UNIT 2: SPY TRAINING

72   *Social and Emotional Curriculum for Gifted Students, Grade 4* © Prufrock Press Inc.

NAME: _____ DATE: _____

Handout 2.4: What's in Your Pockets? *continued*

Use the analysis you made on the previous page to create items that represent each personal trait you cited. Each of these items must actually fit inside a person's pocket.

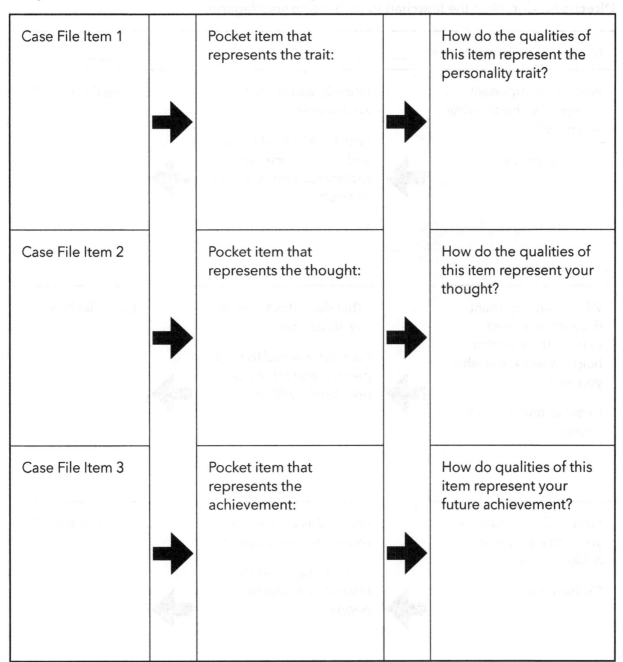

Craft the three items above and place them in your evidence bag. The evidence bag goes with your case file. Your legacy is complete as soon as you begin living it.

NAME: _____ DATE: _____

Handout 2.4

What's in Your Pockets? Sample

Directions: Complete the flowchart to help create your legend.

Name (Fake Identity Name): _____				
What is an important personality characteristic you have? *I never give up!*	➡	How do you know? Give an example. *I work really hard to do well. My science fair project took me a month to finish.*	➡	Case File Item 1
What is an important thought you often think—a thought that helps others know who you are? *I want to find a cure for cancer.*	➡	What does this thought say about you? *I am determined to help people, and I don't care how hard it will be.*	➡	Case File Item 2
What will someday be your most important achievement? *Curing cancer!*	➡	How is this achievement related to your legacy? *I want to be known as a kind person who helped people.*	➡	Case File Item 3

‹ UNIT 2: SPY TRAINING ›

74 *Social and Emotional Curriculum for Gifted Students, Grade 4* © Prufrock Press Inc.

NAME: _____ DATE: _____

Handout 2.4: What's in Your Pockets? Sample, *continued*

Use the analysis you made on the previous page to create items that represent each personal trait you cited. Each of these items must actually fit inside a person's pocket.

Case File Item 1	➡	Pocket item that represents the trait: *Ants*	➡	How do the qualities of this item represent the personality trait? *These little guys are known for never giving up and for helping their colony survive in any way they can.*
Case File Item 2	➡	Pocket item that represents the thought: *Safety pin*	➡	How do the qualities of this item represent your thought? *This handy item is helpful in a thousand ways.*
Case File Item 3	➡	Pocket item that represents the achievement: *Bandage*	➡	How do qualities of this item represent your future achievement? *Bandages heal and protect.*

Craft the three items above and place them in your evidence bag. The evidence bag goes with your case file. Your legacy is complete as soon as you begin living it.

Lesson 2.5

Award Certificate and Diary

Students will imagine details about their future, creating an award certificate and a "hopes and dreams" diary entry to help them envision success.

Materials

- » Handout 2.5: Doubts and Fears Diary
- » Construction or scrapbooking paper
- » Pens, markers, colored pencils, etc.

Estimated Time

- » 30–40 minutes

Procedure

Award Certificate. Have students create an award certificate for themselves that they might win sometime in the future. They should make sure that the certificate realistically matches their personalities, skills, and talents. Share these guidelines:
- » The award certificate should be an actual award that students could win someday.
- » It should be an award that helps prove students are using their talents and abilities on their way to a successful career in the future.
- » On the back of the certificate, they should write 3–5 sentences explaining why they've chosen to create this award certificate.

> **Figure 10**
> Award Certificate Example

See the sample from Steven Jackson in Figure 10. Doesn't it make sense that someone who dreams of curing cancer someday would win a middle school science fair along the way? *Note.* This certificate looks pretty polished because a big stack of scrapbooking paper was donated to my classroom. Is it possible to bring fancy paper from home or elsewhere to use with this lesson?

Doubts and Fears Diary. Share Handout 2.5: Doubts and Fears Diary with students. This handout will help students see that success often goes hand in hand with doubts and fears. Every person has challenges that help them learn and grow. Figure 11 shows an example of a diary entry.

Figure 11
Diary Example

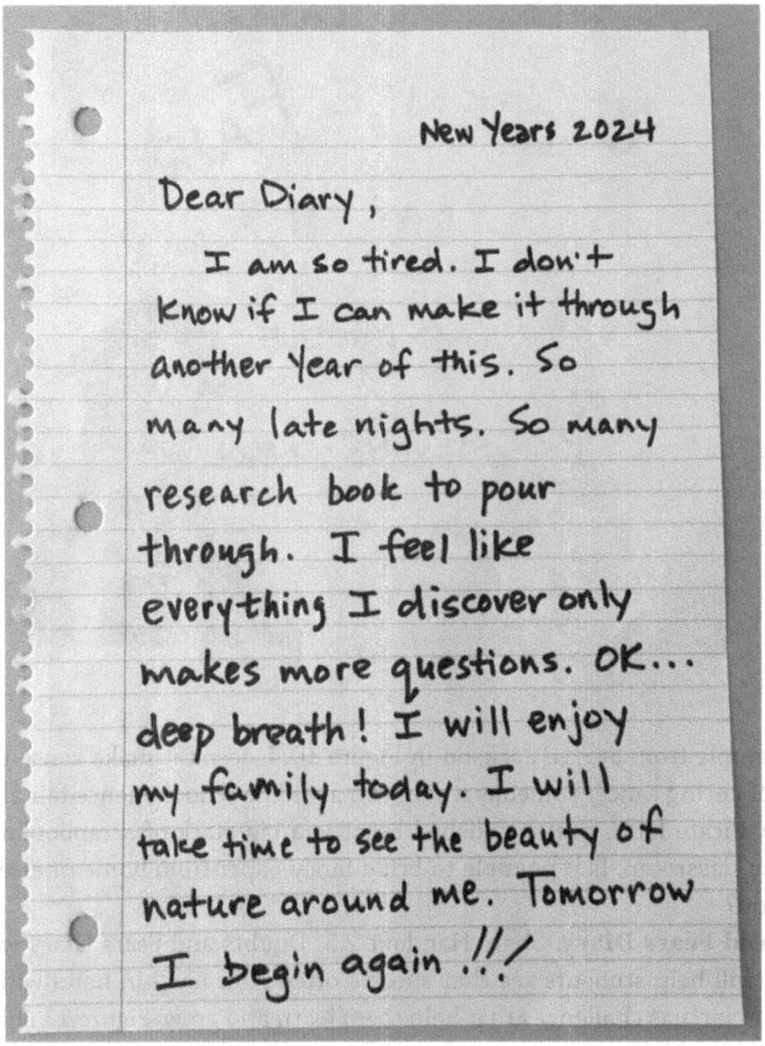

> New Years 2024
>
> Dear Diary,
>
> I am so tired. I don't know if I can make it through another year of this. So many late nights. So many research book to pour through. I feel like everything I discover only makes more questions. OK... deep breath! I will enjoy my family today. I will take time to see the beauty of nature around me. Tomorrow I begin again.!!/

NAME: _____ DATE: _____

Handout 2.5
Doubts and Fears Diary

A tattered and torn diary page describing your doubts and fears has been found in your belongings. As an expert spy, you knew all about it and wanted it to be found! It will only make your cover identity and legend even more real.

How could a person so successful in life have doubts and fears, you ask? Everyone has doubts and fears. Everyone has challenges. The larger the goal, the larger the challenge. Everyone gets discouraged from time to time. These things are a natural part of living and dreaming and doing and growing.

Directions: On a separate page or the back on this handout, consider the following questions and create a diary entry to include with the rest of your spy materials:

- » What doubts and fears might your future self have? Make these fit your future life and achievements or failures.
- » What external conflicts are causing the doubts and fears?
- » What internal conflicts are causing the doubts and fears?
- » What will your future self do to lessen the doubts and fears?
- » Date the entry accurately based on your legend and cover identity.
- » Remember, a diary always reflects the personality of its creator. Would the handwriting be fine or sloppy? Would there be doodles and diagrams?

Social and Emotional Curriculum for Gifted Students, Grade 4 © Prufrock Press Inc.

UNIT 3

Antibullying Intervention
Empathy and Justice

Background

Enhance your school's antibullying curriculum with these creative, challenging social-emotional lessons with connections to standards. In this unit, students create an antibullying invention, elaborate with details and a clear focus, and then participate in a standards-based speaking and listening activity through a kid-friendly extemporaneous speech. With this unit, students synthesize ideas and skills for success both inside the classroom and on the playground.

Bullying and its consequences are, or will be, a part of every student's experience in one way or another. In addition, education about bullying is especially fitting as a part of social-emotional instruction for gifted learners for several reasons:

» Gifted learners can be especially sensitive to social interactions around them—even more so if they have gifted intensities or overexcitabilities.
» Gifted learners tend to have a strong sense of justice, which makes education about bullying poignant for them.
» Many of our gifted learners have the potential to become strong leaders, and all school leaders should be aware of bullying. Many of our gifted learners have the tools

to step in and make appropriate responses to situations in which they encounter bullying personally or as a bystander.
- » Some of our gifted learners do not fit in very well at school or with same-age peers. If this is a case, they might become bullying targets.

Unit Objectives

Students will:
- » understand bullying and its consequences, and
- » equip themselves with ways to proactively stop bullying.

NAGC Learning and Development Standard

1.5. Cognitive, Psychosocial, and Affective Growth. Students with gifts and talents demonstrate cognitive growth and psychosocial skills that support their talent development as a result of meaningful and challenging learning activities that address their unique characteristics and needs.

Themes and Skills Addressed

Social-Emotional Themes
- » Bullying
- » Social problem solving

Academic Skills
- » Extemporaneous speaking
- » Graphic design
- » Building and engineering

Launch

Show the video "The Short Story of a Fox and a Mouse–ESMA 2015" (https://www.youtube.com/watch?v=k6kCwj0Sk4s). This short animated video gives students much to contemplate. Although the video is not a bullying story, per se, it can be used to form a mental set and to discuss some of the themes that surround bullying. Answers to the following questions will vary:
- » Near the end of the video, why do you think the fox looks menacingly at the birds?
- » This video makes use of situational irony (where we expect one thing to happen, but instead, an unexpected event occurs). What are some examples of this?
- » Although this video is not really about bullying, we can make some connections between the fox/mouse and bullies/victims. What are some of these connections?

» At the beginning of this video, the birds play the part of bystanders. What is a bystander in a bullying situation?
» What actions could the birds have taken to help the mouse? Why do you think they did not take these actions?

Note. This launch exercise can be found in a different format as part of my KidVidThink Daily collection—lessons that use short videos to engage students in critical thinking exercises and optional in-depth extension activities. The KidVidThink Daily collection is available free from my website at https://www.giftedlearners.org/projects-2.

Lesson 3.1

Antibullying Inventions

Many schools already follow an antibullying curriculum, and this lesson will work alongside these resources and curriculum. General social-emotional curriculums and programs designed for all ages and ability levels typically fail to address the needs of gifted learners. By participating in this unit, gifted students will benefit from an in-depth examination of issues and be challenged with a creative project that enhances the general curricular experience.

Materials

- Handout 3.1: Antibullying Invention Rubric
- Containers of various sizes: Clear out toy boxes, junk drawers, the garage, and the recycle bin to gather all sorts of boxes, containers, or kid's meal toys. Cut them up. Tear them apart. These will be the building blocks of students' inventions.
- Other suggested materials (pick and choose as needed):
  - Dowels
  - Wooden wheels
  - Cardstock
  - Markers
  - Tape
  - Low-temperature mini hot glue guns
  - Glue
  - Paper clips
  - Pipe cleaners
  - Craft sticks
  - Aluminum foil
  - Paper towel and toilet paper tubes
  - 2-liter bottles
  - Other common classroom or craft items you can find

Unit 3: Antibullying Intervention

Estimated Time

At least 2 hours. Time will vary depending on the craft items available and the pace of students' work. Allow ample time for the creative building process. You will notice that the class's synergy begins to generate some amazing and delightful inventions if you allow the gift of time in your classroom workshop.

Preparation

It may be both fun and useful to create your own antibullying device in advance of teaching this unit so that you may model the building and crafting process (Lesson 3.1) as well as the extemporaneous speaking process (Lesson 3.3). Take a look at the examples shared in this lesson to determine what kind of device you'd like to create.

Procedure

In this first activity, students are introduced to the invention task and view samples as well as a rubric for evaluation.

Introduce the task: Students must invent a device that will prevent, deter, or stop bullying. This invention may not cause anyone harm in any way. Explain to students that they don't want to hurt bullies; they just want to stop them and/or teach them a lesson. This invention doesn't really have to *work* or be practical. Students should use their imaginations to make something fun and cool that will "get the job done." In fact, a sense of humor is preferred.

Share Handout 3.1: Antibullying Invention Rubric to help guide students to create a successful invention. Three sample inventions from fourth-grade students can be found in Figure 12:

» The first invention is a "bully stopper" remote control with an antenna that can be extended or shortened depending on how far away the bully stands. A selection of "flip out" cards sends different clear messages to the bully, like "Stop!" or "I don't like how you are treating me."

» The next invention is a remote control that sends out a forcefield that ensnares bullies in a cage-like device. Just press the big red button. After all, what's an electronic device without a big red button? And just look how unhappy the bully is . . .

» The third invention is a rocket ship that happily and safely suspends the potential victim (see the rubber bands?) in a protective shield. It blasts them far away to safety. Look at the steam and flaming fuel emitted from the bottom!

Figure 12
Antibullying Invention Examples

"Bully stopper" remote control.

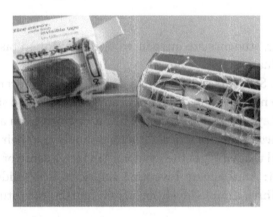

Forcefield device.

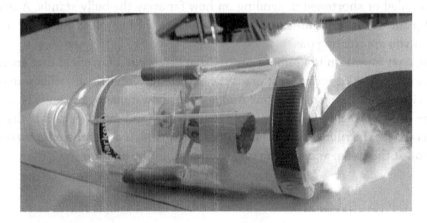

Protective rocket ship.

NAME:_____ DATE: _____

Handout 3.1
Antibullying Invention Rubric

Advanced	Proficient	In Progress
This invention is clearly designed (along with an explanation) to prevent bullying from happening, to stop it if it does happen, or to teach a bully a valuable lesson.	This is an invention about bullying, but it is not always clear what purpose it will serve. It might be just creative, funny, or cool. It needs a stronger purpose.	It is not clear how this invention will prevent bullying, stop it, or teach any valuable lessons.
This invention has moving or working parts and/or complicated constructions. It must have been challenging to design and build and may even be a working prototype.	This invention is a good model. The inventor made good choices for materials that represent the different parts of the model. The model has all of the important parts and might also have interesting details as well.	This invention is unfinished, or important parts are missing from the model.
The designer took time to make this neat and attractive in appearance. It not only does its job with a bully, but also looks good. If someone saw it in an advertisement, they would want to buy it.	It looks like some parts should be bigger or smaller—like it doesn't quite fit together correctly. Mostly, the invention is well-built and doesn't need many adjustments.	The invention falls apart, or pieces are missing. Back to the workshop! More time needed.

Notes:

Lesson 3.2

Preparing an Antibullying Speech

Once students have completed their invention, they will prepare for a speaking and listening activity. Nobody can lose focus and talk (and talk and talk) like some of the elementary students in gifted and talented classes, so this lesson provides students with a focus and a format to give a kid-friendly extemporaneous speech.

Materials

- » Handout 3.2: Public Speaking Template
- » Handout 3.2: Public Speaking Template Sample
- » Antibullying invention models

Estimated Time

- » 20–30 minutes

Procedure

Share with students some notes on effective public speaking. Excellent public speakers do not memorize; instead, effective speakers present from notes (extemporaneous speaking). These notes help students focus on what they will share about their invention and limit what will be shared. Reluctant speakers feel prepared as well, and their anxiety will be eased as they share their inventions.

Share Handout 3.2: Public Speaking Template to help students prepare for speeches. In this activity, students are asked to focus on a key feature of their invention (i.e., What is the main idea you will share?). The key sections of the speech include the following:

Unit 3: Antibullying Intervention

1. First, students select a name for their invention.
2. Students cite whether the invention is to deter, prevent, or stop bullying.
3. Next, students focus on a main feature. Our 21st-century learners rely on visual avenues and nonverbal ability like no generation before them. That's why students will begin by drawing an "ultra close-up" of their key feature. By drawing this feature, students consider its component details and create their own speaking and writing context and content.
4. Students write key descriptive words they will use in their presentations. Word choice and language variety are sometimes difficult challenges. Encourage students to choose words that will make their descriptions interesting. Don't allow students to write out the description in complete sentences—you want them to speak from notes.
5. Finally, students explain the importance of their key feature. It's OK to write complete sentences here but not absolutely necessary. More reluctant speakers should write more in this area to reduce their anxiety. Students aren't focusing on delivery as much as content, so it's no problem if a student wants to read this last part word for word when they present their inventions.

Handout 3.2: Public Speaking Template Sample shares a student invention, the Bullianator, used to stop bullying.

NAME: _____ DATE: _____

Handout 3.2
Public Speaking Template

Directions: Complete the following questions to help you identify the most important information for your extemporaneous speech.

---

1. Opening: What is the name of your invention?

---

2. Category: Is your invention used to deter, stop, or prevent bullying?

---

3. Zoom in! Draw your invention's most important or innovative feature close up. Super-size it.

---

4. Look at your drawing. What words will describe the most important feature of your invention?

---

5. Explain why this feature is so important.

NAME:_____ DATE: _____

Handout 3.2
Public Speaking Template Sample

Directions: Complete the following questions to help you identify the most important information for your extemporaneous speech.

---

1. Opening: What is the name of your invention?

   The Bullianator

---

2. Category: Is your invention used to deter, stop, or prevent bullying?

   Stop

---

3. Zoom in! Draw your invention's most important or innovative feature close up. Super-size it.

---

4. Look at your drawing. What words will describe the most important feature of your invention?

   Slingshot web, target activated, capture button

---

5. Explain why this feature is so important.

   The main reason for the Bullianator is to shoot a web at the bully so you can take them to the principal's office.

Lesson 3.3

Delivering the Antibullying Speech

Having identified the main components of their antibullying inventions, students are now prepared to deliver the speech to their classmates.

Materials

- » Handout 3.2: Public Speaking Template
- » Antibullying invention models

Estimated Time

- » Timing depends upon the size of your class. Keep in mind that extemporaneous speeches should be short—certainly less than 2 minutes each.

Preparation

Prepare a sample speech to model your expectations for students. This speech can reference the sample bullying device you created if applicable (see Preparation section in Lesson 3.1).

Procedure

Having completed Handout 3.2: Public Speaking Template, students are prepared to deliver the speech to their classmates—with one added skill. Encourage students to refer to specific components of their invention when speaking—pointing, for example, to a big red

Unit 3: Antibullying Intervention

activation button on their device as they explain the button's function. This is a part of typical academic standards in public speaking. It's a good idea to model your expectations with an extemporaneous speech of your own.

My class does not rehearse these speeches, but it certainly wouldn't hurt to do so. If I have successfully created a space where students feel safe and accepted, I've found that students do just fine without the rehearsal.

Because common academic public speaking standards include a listening component, ask a question or two to the audience members after each speech. This reinforces the importance of good, courteous listening skills. Questions such as, "What was the most important feature of McKenzie's invention?" and "What was one detail about the invention you found interesting?" help support writing standards, even if the responses are oral. In my classroom, the antibullying inventions are an ungraded activity. I make sure to provide one statement of positive feedback after each speech and also invite *one* positive comment from a classmate, written or oral. Each speech—including questions and feedback—should only last a couple of minutes.

The following is a sample of what might be said in the extemporaneous speech related to the antibullying invention shown in Handout 3.2: Public Speaking Template Sample:

> My invention is the Bullianator.
> It STOPS bullying in its tracks.
> The Bullianator's main feature is the slingshot web. When you see bullying happening, just check the viewscreen and sight in your target. When your target is activated, press the "capture" button. A web comes slinging out of the Bullianator and traps the criminal bully. Once they are ensnared in the web, simply take the bully straight to the principal's office!

UNIT 4

Penguin Problems
Ownership and Accountability

Background

"He cut in front of me!" Ever heard that one in a school?

"No fair!" How about that one?

In a gifted mind and body full of intensities, anything can loom, disastrous. Gifted learners—whose asynchronous development might have them thinking like a 14-year-old but living in a social world of a first grader—might need some practice with the sort of executive functioning that helps them intercept thoughts and feelings before they balloon and pop. Let's help them learn how to let go of *penguin problems*.

What are penguin problems? Minor issues, minor inconveniences, and silly concerns, penguin problems are not even problems at all. Are your students driving you crazy with petty issues and their own penguin problems? They need to take ownership—enough penguin problems, already!

In addition to critical thinking and problem solving around social and personal issues in this lesson, students learn a bit of language etymology, practice poetic writing with strong word choice, examine metaphors, and exercise critical thinking skills.

Social and Emotional Curriculum for Gifted Students Grade 4

Unit Objectives

Students will:
- » recognize when a problem is actually a problem rather than a minor disruption or inconvenience, and
- » practice solving minor social and personal issues.

NAGC Learning and Development Standards

1.1. Self-Understanding. Students with gifts and talents recognize their interests, strengths, and needs in cognitive, creative, social, emotional, and psychological areas.

1.3. Self-Understanding. Students with gifts and talents demonstrate understanding of and respect for similarities and differences between themselves and their cognitive and chronological peer groups and others in the general population.

1.5. Cognitive, Psychosocial, and Affective Growth. Students with gifts and talents demonstrate cognitive growth and psychosocial skills that support their talent development as a result of meaningful and challenging learning activities that address their unique characteristics and needs.

Themes and Skills Addressed

Social-Emotional Themes
- » Resilience
- » Executive functioning
- » Perfectionism
- » Gratitude
- » Social problem solving
- » Psychosocial development

Academic Skills
- » Vocabulary in context
- » Theme
- » Etymology
- » Characterization
- » Word choice

Launch

"Dinner From Birdbox Studio" is a delightful short animation: https://www.youtube.com/watch?v=Rp30_gF1GcY. Show the video and discuss the following questions with the

Unit 4: Penguin Problems

class. As students share ideas, they will build a preview for problem solving and the emotions associated with it. Answers will vary:
- » What is the dog's first reaction to its problem? Do people sometimes do the same thing? Give an example.
- » What would have happened if the dog had panicked?
- » Would it have been better if the dog had waited for its owner to come along and solve the problem?
- » Describe the feelings of the dog during this video. How do the feelings change from the beginning to the end?
- » One message this video may be sending is that as soon as we feel like we have solved a little problem in life, another one is sure to come along. Do you agree with this observation? Why or why not?

Lesson 4.1

Penguin Problems

In the first lesson of this unit, the class will read aloud the book *Penguin Problems*, identify its theme, and establish a shared meaning for penguin problems.

Materials

- » Handout 4.1: Penguin Problems Theme
- » Teacher copy of *Penguin Problems* by Jory John, illustrated by Lane Smith

Estimated Time

- » 30 minutes

Procedure

To begin, read the book *Penguin Problems* by Jory John and Lane Smith aloud with the class and arrive at a consensus for a definition of a penguin problem. State the theme of the book as the anchor point for this unit.

Share Handout 4.1: Penguin Problems Theme. You may prefer to have students complete this activity as an individual assignment, as a think-pair-share, or with the entire group as a discussion activity. My class used think-pair-share in a full classroom, and it worked well. You want students to open a discussion about the theme and then naturally begin to discuss the possible outcomes of penguin problems in the real world. Students should understand this theme: *Some people focus on problems that are not really problems at all, while forgetting about all of the things they might be thankful for.*

Unit 4: Penguin Problems

As a follow-up, ask students to point out details that support the theme. The penguin, for example, chooses to focus on annoyances he can't control, like the sun being too bright or the fact that he cannot fly. He fails to see the beauty of the ocean, feel the warm sun on his shoulders, and enjoy the companionship of those who love him.

99

NAME:_____ DATE:_____

Handout 4.1
Penguin Problems Theme

Directions: Themes are much bigger than the story itself. Themes are observations that authors share about the world. The story's characters behave in certain ways to help us understand the observation. By watching how characters react to a story's events, we can figure out a story's theme. What is the theme of *Penguin Problems*? Consider what happens in the story. Ask yourself, "What is a penguin problem anyway?"

> **Theme**
> » A theme is a major idea in a story, poem, or novel.
> » A theme is meaningful even outside of the story. It's an observation about the way things are.
> » A theme is something important an author is trying to say.

Write one sentence below that you think captures the theme of *Penguin Problems*. Be prepared to share your idea with the class:

Lesson 4.2

Penguin Problem as a Metaphor

In this lesson, students discuss how the penguin problem can be aptly connected to a penguin itself. This is a good exercise in critical thinking, creativity, and understanding of metaphors. Students also consider the etymology of the phrase *lay an egg*.

Materials

- » Handout 4.2: Penguin Problems Metaphor
- » Handout 4.2: Penguin Problems Metaphor Sample
- » Handout 4.2: Lay an Egg
- » Handout 4.2: Lay an Egg Sample

Estimated Time

- » 30 minutes

Procedure

Penguin Metaphors. Tell students: *Let's discuss how the penguin problem can be aptly connected to a penguin itself. This will be a good exercise in critical thinking, creativity, and understanding of metaphors.*

Share Handout 4.2: Penguin Problems Metaphor with students. You may prefer to complete this activity as a group discussion. Students will connect the qualities of actual penguins with the idea of penguin problems. Sample answers can be found on the page following the handout.

Social and Emotional Curriculum for Gifted Students Grade 4

Etymology. Once the class has identified relevant penguin problems, transition into the etymology portion of this lesson. Because the class penguin will be "laying eggs" in a later activity, this is a perfect segue (one which was started with the metaphors). Tell students: *We will examine the idiom "laying an egg" with critical and metaphorical thinking.*

Distribute Handout 4.2: Lay an Egg and have students consider the questions about etymology and idioms. This is a good activity for pairs or groups of three. Sample answers can be found on the page following the handout.

NAME: _____ DATE: _____

Handout 4.2

Penguin Problems Metaphor

Directions: Well, well, well . . . it seems that a penguin is a perfect metaphor for "penguin problems." Metaphors are figures of speech comparing two things that share certain qualities. For example, "My brother is a bear in the morning!" Let's connect penguins and penguin problems using the graphic organizer below. Think about qualities that real-life penguins share with penguin problems. The first connection is completed for you.

Penguin Quality	Penguin Problem
A penguin is an awkward walker.	*Penguins look kind of silly, but that's the way they are, and they can't change. Penguin problems are often silly, and we can't change them. We need to just deal with them!*
Penguins make squawking sounds.	
A penguin will stand for countless hours protecting its eggs.	

UNIT 4: PENGUIN PROBLEMS

Social and Emotional Curriculum for Gifted Students, Grade 4 © Prufrock Press Inc.

NAME:_____ DATE: _____

Handout 4.2

Penguin Problems Metaphor Sample

Directions: Well, well, well . . . it seems that a penguin is a perfect metaphor for "penguin problems." Metaphors are figures of speech comparing two things that share certain qualities. For example, "My brother is a bear in the morning!" Let's connect penguins and penguin problems using the graphic organizer below. Think about qualities that real-life penguins share with penguin problems. The first connection is completed for you.

Penguin Quality	Penguin Problem
A penguin is an awkward walker.	*Penguins look kind of silly, but that's the way they are, and they can't change. Penguin problems are often silly, and we can't change them. We need to just deal with them!*
Penguins make squawking sounds.	*People who always complain about little problems they can't do anything about are like squawking birds. All it becomes is an annoying clatter, and you just wish they would be quiet. When everyone is squawking, it's deafening!*
A penguin will stand for countless hours protecting its eggs.	*People just won't let these little problems go sometimes. They protect them and hover over them like they're baby chicks. If they woke up and thought about it, they'd realize these problems are as easily broken as an egg.*

NAME:_____ DATE:_____

Handout 4.2

Lay an Egg

Directions: "Lay an egg" is an idiom or figure of speech. It means to fail, flop, or not complete what was meant to be done. For example: *During the school musical, Sally laid an egg when she forgot her lines.* Consider the following questions about idioms.

1. What is another example of an idiom?

2. To understand how the idiom "lay an egg" originated, think about eggs. List an egg's qualities.

3. As early as 1863, British cricket teams that failed to score a run were said to have "laid a duck's egg." American baseball teams that don't score in an inning are said to "put a goose egg up on the scoreboard." Now think about it. Why is failing to score a run in cricket or baseball called a duck egg or goose egg?

4. Why is failing at something called "laying an egg"?

NAME: _____ DATE: _____

Handout 4.2

Lay an Egg Sample

Directions: "Lay an egg" is an idiom or figure of speech. It means to fail, flop, or not complete what was meant to be done. For example: *During the school musical, Sally laid an egg when she forgot her lines.* Consider the following questions about idioms.

1. What is another example of an idiom?

    He missed the boat. She got cold feet.

2. To understand how the idiom "lay an egg" originated, think about eggs. List an egg's qualities.

    Oval, round, has liquid and yolk inside, brown or speckled or white, fragile, contains a baby, laid by birds, we eat them

3. As early as 1863, British cricket teams that failed to score a run were said to have "laid a duck's egg." American baseball teams that don't score in an inning are said to "put a goose egg up on the scoreboard." Now think about it. Why is failing to score a run in cricket or baseball called a duck egg or goose egg?

    Because it is zero points. A zero looks like an egg on the scoreboard.

4. Why is failing at something called "laying an egg"?

    Failing is like scoring zero runs in cricket.

Lesson 4.3

Penguin Solutions

We've made it to the brainstorming and solutions portion of the unit, in which students generate ideas for solving penguin problems. Arguably, this lesson requires the most critical thinking—and as such, it will hopefully stick with students.

Materials

- » Lesson 4.3: Penguin Solutions
- » Lesson 4.3: Penguin Solutions Sample
- » Penguin display materials:
  - » Scissors (one pair per student)
  - » Tape
  - » A poster maker (or a teacher skilled in drawing) to create a drawing of a penguin and eggs

Estimated Time

- » 30 minutes

Procedure

Distribute Handout 4.3: Penguin Solutions for students to generate ideas for problem solving. Students will describe a penguin problem and then brainstorm possible ways this problem can be dealt with. Although the lesson might begin as an individual assignment, make sure to allow for a lot of interaction with this problem-solving activity. Once students

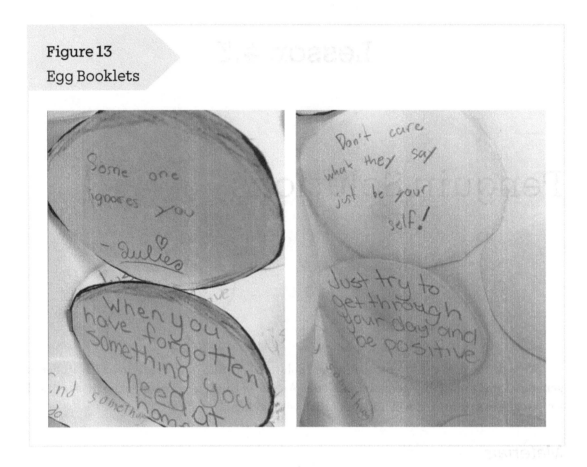

Figure 13
Egg Booklets

have considered their solutions, encourage them to share their ideas with classmates. Sample answers can be found on the page following the handout.

Once students have created their problems and solutions, they will make a little "egg booklet" with the problem on the egg's "cover" and a solution inside. See Figure 13 for two examples, with problems on the left and solutions on the right.

When the eggs are completed, display them on the wall for everyone to see. See Figure 14 for a display created in my classroom using a poster maker. Select volunteers who would like to share the problems and solutions with the entire class. The class is apt to fill up with smiles and nodding of heads as students share their penguin problems. Many students will have experienced the same problems: "Yep! I've been there and done that one myself!" Hearing that others experience the same sorts of minor issues and have lived to tell about it creates community in your classroom.

Figure 14
Penguin Problems and Solutions Display

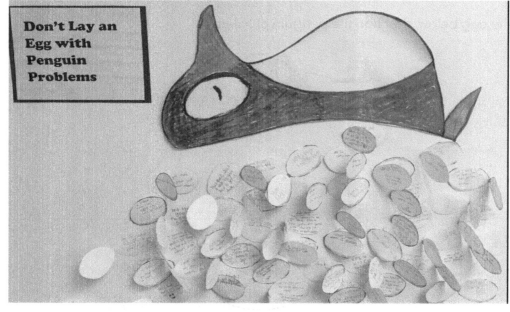

NAME: _____ DATE: _____

Handout 4.3

Penguin Solutions

Directions: For goodness sakes! Somebody laid an egg and is experiencing a penguin problem of the first order. Let's give them some advice to help.

In the egg below, describe the penguin problem.

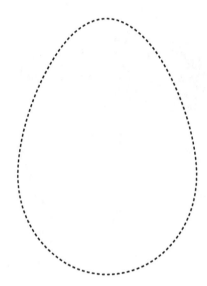

In the second egg, offer advice for how to solve the problem. We can't have all of these eggs lying around here!

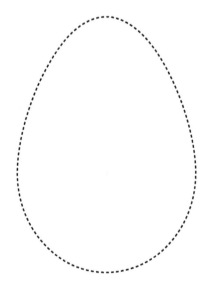

Construction
To assemble your eggs, cut them out on the dotted lines. Then, tape the first egg (the problem) on top of the second egg (the solution), with the tape on the left side. When you open the egg, your advice can be found inside.

NAME: _____ DATE: _____

Handout 4.3

Penguin Solutions Sample

Directions: For goodness sakes! Somebody laid an egg and is experiencing a penguin problem of the first order. Let's give them some advice to help.

In the egg below, describe the penguin problem.

Forgetting a jacket at recess when it's chilly outside.

In the second egg, offer advice for how to solve the problem. We can't have all of these eggs lying around here!

Ask your teacher courteously to go inside to get your jacket. If the answer is no, then just deal with it. You are not going to freeze to death in 15 minutes. You won't forget your jacket next time!

Construction
To assemble your eggs, cut them out on the dotted lines. Then, tape the first egg (the problem) on top of the second egg (the solution), with the tape on the left side. When you open the egg, your advice can be found inside.

Social and Emotional Curriculum for Gifted Students, Grade 4 © Prufrock Press Inc.

Lesson 4.4

Gratitude: Listen to the Walrus

Fortunately, in the book *Penguin Problems*, the walrus emerges to remind the penguin and readers that we have plenty in life to feel grateful about. This final lesson in Unit 4 invites students to think about and share gratitude.

Materials

- » Handout 4.4: Walrus Gratitude
- » Handout 4.4: Walrus Gratitude Sample
- » Teacher copy of *Penguin Problems* by Jory John, illustrated by Lane Smith

Estimated Time

- » 20 minutes

Procedure

As a class, reread the walrus section from *Penguin Problems*, in which the walrus reminds readers that it is easy to lose sight of gratitude while focusing on penguin problems.

Distribute Handout 4.4: Walrus Gratitude and invite students to reflect on gratitude. As students write about what they are grateful for, they should consider using poetic descriptions, careful word choice, and thoughtful, creative wordsmithing. To help students focus on their word choice, share the sample answer page following the handout. Have students underline creative and skilled word choices that this student made.

Once students have completed their messages, consider how you would like to share them with the class or the rest of the school. My school uses Capturing Kids' Hearts, a social-emotional program (see https://www.capturingkidshearts.org/training/teachers-and-campus-staff/ckh1). A big part of this program is recognizing the people and things for which we are all grateful, so discussing these messages of gratitude during morning classroom meetings is a ready-made way to share. Perhaps your class would like to share these messages verbally, collect them into a class publication, or post them on the wall as a companion to the penguin problems display.

NAME: _____   DATE: _____

Handout 4.4
Walrus Gratitude

Directions: In *Penguin Problems*, the walrus reminds us that it is easy to lose sight of all of the good things in life—no matter how simple they may be—if we are always focused on penguin problems. What is something you are thankful and grateful for? Describe what you are thankful and grateful for using your best walrus-like word choice: poetic, vivid, and detailed.

NAME:_____ DATE:_____

Handout 4.4
Walrus Gratitude Sample

Directions: In *Penguin Problems*, the walrus reminds us that it is easy to lose sight of all of the good things in life—no matter how simple they may be—if we are always focused on penguin problems. What is something you are thankful and grateful for? Describe what you are thankful and grateful for using your best walrus-like word choice: poetic, vivid, and detailed.

> *I am thankful and grateful for sunlit winter mornings. As we stand huddled in our coats waiting to enter the school, the sun peers over the houses in the neighborhood and finds us waiting with our icy breath swirling into the air. The sun then stretches our long shadows in front of us playfully. "Here I am! Let me warm you. Greet the day!"*

UNIT 4: PENGUIN PROBLEMS

UNIT 5

Our Colorful Selves
Personality and Giftedness

Background

The value in this collection of lessons is the opportunity for personal reflection, informal conversations about the nature of giftedness in a nonthreatening atmosphere, and a sort of casual, fun design challenge. These conversations and reflections should not be a one-time, once-a-year lesson. You might use this unit midyear in your classroom or start with this unit in your gifted classroom at the beginning of the year if need be. I use these lessons with fourth graders midyear as we return to our earlier discussions about giftedness, but it will help in an introduction to giftedness as well. Although this unit is designed for fourth grade, it can also be adapted to work with just about any age from primary to adult.

Although the concepts may seem simple, this social-emotional unit is full of critical thinking, personal reflection, and considerations of what it means to be gifted. It's great for students who love language arts and math, and it will appeal to those with general intellectual abilities and nonverbal abilities alike.

Social and Emotional Curriculum for Gifted Students Grade 4

Unit Objectives

Students will:
- » understand their personal qualities and how they intersect to form a unique individual,
- » cite details that connect them to another person, and
- » explore what it means to be a gifted learner.

NAGC Learning and Development Standards

1.1. Self-Understanding. Students with gifts and talents recognize their interests, strengths, and needs in cognitive, creative, social, emotional, and psychological areas.

1.3. Self-Understanding. Students with gifts and talents demonstrate understanding of and respect for similarities and differences between themselves and their cognitive and chronological peer groups and others in the general population.

1.5. Cognitive, Psychosocial, and Affective Growth. Students with gifts and talents demonstrate cognitive growth and psychosocial skills that support their talent development as a result of meaningful and challenging learning activities that address their unique characteristics and needs.

Themes and Skills Addressed

Social-Emotional Themes
- » Friendship
- » Identity
- » Perfectionism
- » Resilience
- » Compassion
- » Psychosocial development
- » Achievement
- » What is giftedness?

Academic Skills
- » Geometry
- » Using measurement and drafting tools
- » Graphic design
- » Metaphor creation
- » Metaphor analysis
- » Collaborative discussion

Unit 5: Our Colorful Selves

Launch

Before beginning the lessons in this unit, review some background information on giftedness with students. Review whatever lessons you've used in the past to explain this concept (see Unit 1 in the previous book in this series, *Social and Emotional Curriculum for Gifted Students: Grade 3*, for an example). Alternately, the following are great discussion points to start the giftedness conversation in your classroom.

Emphasize two things to your young gifted learners:
1. Giftedness says nothing about our personality and the way we treat others. Think of all of the evil villains who must also be gifted learners! We *choose* to be kind, good friends, generous, trustworthy, modest, forgiving, etc.
2. Being identified as a gifted learner is about what we *can* do (our abilities). What we *choose* to do with our giftedness is up to us. We can choose to work hard and accept challenges. We can choose to try more difficult projects and to keep trying even if we don't succeed.

Lesson 5.1

Drawing With a Compass

This lesson beings with a bit of graphic design or mechanical drawing. This approach will engage all learners right away, but especially your quantitative, general intellectual, and nonverbally gifted students.

Materials

- » Compasses (one per student)
- » Rulers (one per student)
- » 8.5" x 11" or 9" x 12" white construction paper
- » Tape

Estimated Time

- » 15–20 minutes

Preparation

If your students are inexperienced with compasses, I suggest practicing a bit before you start this lesson. I am still frustrated with compasses half the time myself! This frustration, however, will end up being part of the lesson as you encourage small fourth-grade hands to persevere with the compasses.

Procedure

Most fourth graders have not had much practice using a compass before. Start simply by giving each student a white sheet of construction paper and a compass. Show students how to set their compasses to a specific radius with a ruler. They'll need to practice holding the paper down with one hand and drawing a circle with another. Many of my students find it easier to rotate the entire paper instead of the compass. (I do, too, sometimes.)

Keep the conversations going as students work on creating circles. Circulate about the classroom and talk to individual students. Some questions to consider while working include:

- » What is a radius?
- » What is diameter?
- » What is circumference?
- » Are circles more commonly drawn with a compass, a computer program, or a template of some sort?
- » Which way is the easiest?

Tips to help students as they create their circles include:

- » Use construction paper. The compass point will stay in place more easily.
- » Tape the paper to the desk. Although this takes away the "spin the paper instead of the compass technique," it frees up both hands.
- » Before drawing, align the pencil and the compass point evenly and properly—pressing together the compass to its smallest position and lining up the pencil to that point.

Lesson 5.2

Overlapping Circles

Once students have practiced drawing circles, the social-emotional components of this unit begin in earnest. This lesson incorporates conversations about the nature of giftedness as students work to draw overlapping circles.

Materials

- » Compasses (one per student)
- » Rulers (one per student)
- » 8.5" x 11" or 9" x 12" white construction paper
- » Colored pencils

Estimated Time

- » 20 minutes

Procedure

The instructions for creating overlapping circles are simple at this point, but carrying out the instructions will be a bit frustrating—as we want it to be! Have students do the following:
- » Set compasses at a 2 1/2 inch radius.
- » Draw three circles with the compasses. The only rule is that each circle should cross into the other two circles. See Figure 15 for an example.

As students work, circulate around the room, offering tips and encouraging discussion. Students are likely to ask questions like: *Where do we cross the circles? Is this in the right place?*

Unit 5: Our Colorful Selves

Figure 15
Three Overlapping Circles

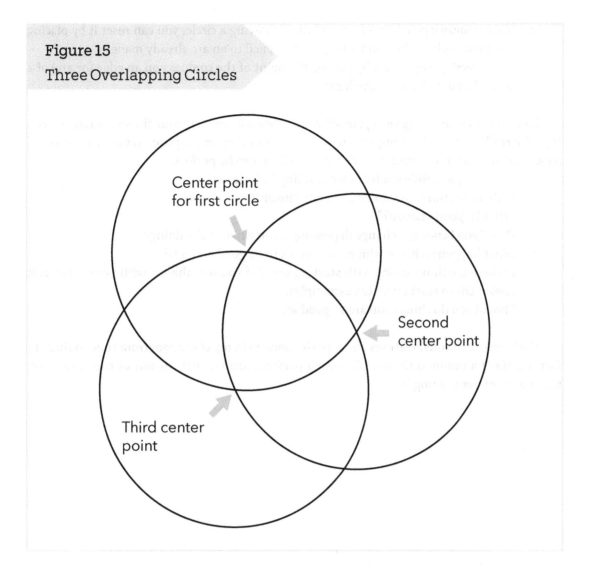

Is this OK? Do the circles have to be perfect? Remind them that the only rule is that **the three circles must cross through each other.**

Here is a great opportunity to talk about relaxing—trusting themselves and learning to thrive even without instructions. Talk about the fact that not all tasks have clear and specific instructions. Does "making friends" have clear and specific instructions? Does giving a hug come with instructions? Can you really fail at something like this? Sometimes students just have to trust their feelings.

Tips for drawing circles include:
» Check each time to make sure the compass is still at 2 1/2 inches.
» Check to make sure your circle will not run off the page by placing the point of the compass down and swinging the pencil across its arc. You will be able to tell if the circle will run off the page.
» Start with the first circle near the top left or top right of the page. This will leave room for the other two.

» If the compass gets "out of whack" while drawing a circle, you can reset it by placing the point back in place and lining up the pencil to an arc already made.
» Make overlapping circles by placing the point of the compass on an edge (or arc) of a circle that has already been drawn.

Draw these circles along with your students. They will see that your circles are not perfect. If you're really good with a compass, mess up your drawing on purpose. Get another sheet of paper and start over. Let students see that it's OK not to be perfect.

Discussion topics while students are working include:
» Is there anything we can do perfectly? Really?
» What is "good enough?"
» Does "good enough" change depending upon what you're doing?
» What happens when nothing ever seems to be good enough?
» Is there anything wrong with starting over? If you're unhappy with your work, is it *always* OK to start over? Give examples.
» Should you do things you aren't good at?

We have casual conversations about perfectionism in my classroom from time to time. In fact, I make it a common theme. Discussing perfectionism casually is one of the most effective means of overcoming it.

Lesson 5.3

What Colors Are You?

This is the heart of our lesson. Students will connect color metaphors to their personal characteristics. This serves not only as an important self-reflective piece, but also as an excellent exercise in metaphorical thinking.

Note. You can find similar color and personality activities in Unit 2 of *Social and Emotional Curriculum for Gifted Students: Grade 3*. My students use similar planning sheets for a variety of activities, including establishing character traits in both biography and fiction. Fourth graders have grown in many ways since the last school year when they may have completed the grade 3 lesson. If you use both lessons, take note of how students' responses have changed and how they have remained the same as well.

Materials

- » Handout 5.3: How Do You Feel About Colors?
- » Handout 5.3: Colors in Me
- » Handout 5.3: Colors in Me Sample
- » Overlapping circle drawings (see Lesson 5.2)
- » Colored pencils: These (not crayons or markers) work best for "blending" characteristics, which students will do in the following lesson.

Estimated Time

- » 30 minutes

Figure 16
Personality Percentages

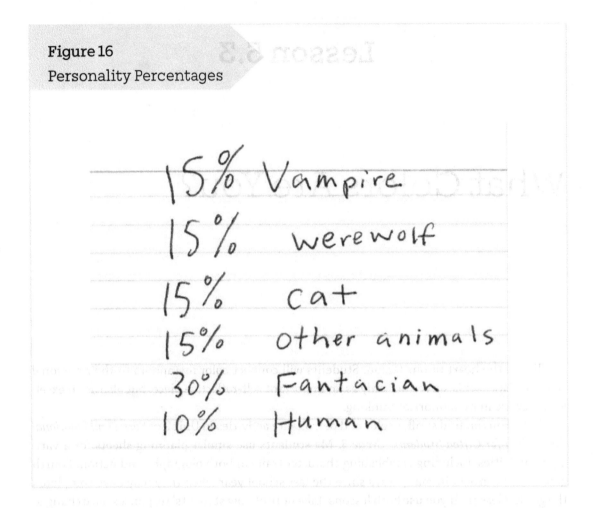

Procedure

Choose Personality Colors. Display the color chart found on Handout 5.3: How Do You Feel About Colors? I have used this chart in several lessons. My class returns to it from time to time for various purposes because color metaphors give a physical, understandable avenue to create and analyze metaphors.

Review the chart and ask students to choose three colors that represent their personalities the best. Distribute Handout 5.3: Colors in Me if needed to help students brainstorm their colors. Sample answers can be found on the page following the handout.

Color Circles. Using colored pencils, have students color the three "uncrossed" portions of the circles they created in Lesson 5.2. As students work, discuss how they are creating a metaphor for themselves with the circles.

I find it amusing to listen to the kids discuss why they choose different colors. As they do so, they are making connections with like-minded others. They see that there is not only one right answer. For example, one highly gifted student came to me with a chart in which she had assigned animal percentages to her personality (see Figure 16). This creative approach was impressive, but her understanding of herself as only "10% human" might reveal something about the feelings that come along with giftedness.

Unit 5: Our Colorful Selves

Share and Discuss. For this lesson, it may be necessary to make sharing more deliberate. Randomly assign students to a group of three to share their color choices and to explain why they've chosen them. Tell students: *Use examples! Let's not forget the importance of supporting opinions with evidence.*

In my classroom, I don't allow students to choose a partner—perhaps in teacher-assigned groups they will meet someone new or learn more about a classmate they don't know very well. I do, however, invite students to do a second round of sharing with whomever they'd like.

Additional discussion questions for the class include:
- How are we all different, even among those who chose the same three colors?
- How are we all alike, even among those whose colors do not match?
- Is it possible to have absolutely nothing in common with someone else?
- Are friendships made only with others who share our personality colors?
- Why is it important in life to understand that different people have different personality colors?

NAME:_____   DATE: _____

Handout 5.3

How Do You Feel About Colors?

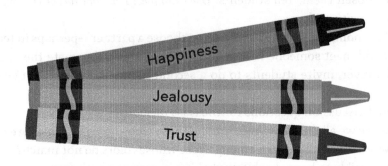

Directions: Read the following passage about colors and consider how different colors make you feel.

Colors make us *think* of certain things, and different colors tend to make us *feel* different ways. Decorators, designers, and advertisers have long used colors and the feelings associated with them for designs. If a decorator wants someone to feel at ease, they will choose a color that feels peaceful and relaxing, like blue. If an advertiser wants someone to see the power of their product, they will choose one of the bold colors that suggest feelings of power, like red.

Sometimes colors make us think of certain things because of what we see around us in nature. Blue makes us think of clear skies—a peaceful feeling. Green makes us think of nature and the living and healthy things in it. Red makes us think of danger. Many poisonous animals, for example, have red colors.

The following are common ways each color can make us feel.

Red excitement, power, energy, love, danger, strength, heat	**Green** nature, jealousy, healthy, lucky, new
Pink love, tenderness, calm, romantic, young	**Purple** spiritual, royal, wise, cruel, mysterious
Yellow hope, friendship, happiness, cowardice, dishonesty	**Black** evil, fear, death, power, elegant, wealthy, mystery
Blue calm, stable, peace, loyalty, sadness, trust	**Gold** wealth, success, luxury, purity
White pure, simple, clean, cold, exact, young	**Orange** social, welcoming, creative, independent, warmhearted

NAME: _____ DATE: _____

Handout 5.3

Colors in Me

Directions: Use Handout 5.3: How Do You Feel About Colors? to match colors that reflect your personality and interests. Use the organizer below to help you explain and provide examples.

Color Matching Your Personality or Interests	Quality Shared by Yourself and the Color	Example or Supporting Story to Explain

NAME:_____ DATE: _____

Handout 5.3

Colors in Me Sample

Directions: Use Handout 5.3: How Do You Feel About Colors? to match colors that reflect your personality and interests. Use the organizer below to help you explain and provide examples.

Color Matching Your Personality or Interests	Quality Shared by Yourself and the Color	Example or Supporting Story to Explain
Blue	Loyalty	Friends are really important to me, and I won't let them down.
Purple	Spiritual	I write poetry, and some people say poems are mystical.
Yellow	Hope	I am always trying to see the good in things and people.

Lesson 5.4

Blending Colors

In this lesson, students reflect on how their personality traits blend together. How do one's traits of a sense of humor and perfectionism, for example, combine for a unique response to a situation? This person may often be able to laugh at themselves in moments of perfectionist frustration.

Materials

- » Handout 5.3: How Do You Feel About Colors?
- » Handout 5.4: Close-Up on Color Blending
- » Handout 5.4: Close-Up on Color Blending Sample
- » Overlapping circle drawings (see previous lessons)
- » Colored pencils

Estimated Time

- » 20 minutes

Procedure

Discuss with the class how personality traits may blend together. Tell students: *We are not just one person, or even three persons. We are many people. We are rich, whole, and complicated individuals who act and react differently in different situations.*

Students will begin by adding to their overlapping circle drawings from the previous lessons. Using the two colored pencils that apply to two of their characteristics, students will blend the two colors together in the portion where the circles cross. They will then repeat this with the other combinations of colors.

Questions to discuss while students are working include:
- » What new color is produced when you blend colors?
- » Is the new color on the color chart (Handout 5.3: How Do You Feel About Colors?)?
- » Does the new color have associated feelings that you sometimes experience?

To help students think more deeply about how their characteristics might blend, have students complete Handout 5.4: Close-Up on Color Blending. In this activity, students consider a specific situation and how their personality aspects might influence their behavior. Sample responses can be found on the page following the handout.

NAME: _____   DATE: _____

Handout 5.4
Close-Up on Color Blending

Directions: Below you will explain how two of your "colors," or aspects of your personality, come together in a situation—how they "blend." Imagine that you are in one of these situations: at school, working on a project, doing a favorite hobby, playing sports, practicing a musical instrument, playing a board game, or at a friend's house. Then, color the circles to represent two aspects of your personality and answer the questions that follow.

Chosen Situation: _____

Two Aspects of Your Personality: _____

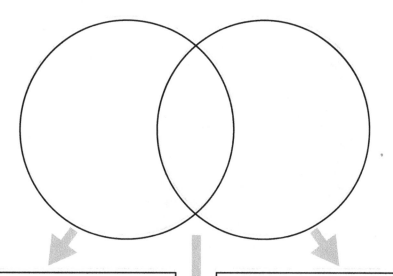

Color 1: If you were acting based on this aspect of your personality, how might you act, or what might you say?

Color 2: If you were acting based on this aspect of your personality, how might you act, or what might you say?

Color Blending: If you were acting based on these two aspects of your personality blending together, how might you act, or what might you say?

Social and Emotional Curriculum for Gifted Students, Grade 4 © Prufrock Press Inc.

NAME:_____ DATE: _____

Handout 5.4

Close-Up on Color Blending Sample

Directions: Below you will explain how two of your "colors," or aspects of your personality, come together in a situation—how they "blend." Imagine that you are in one of these situations: at school, working on a project, doing a favorite hobby, playing sports, practicing a musical instrument, playing a board game, or at a friend's house. Then, color the circles to represent two aspects of your personality and answer the questions that follow.

Chosen Situation: *Playing a board game*

Two Aspects of Your Personality: *Energy and hope*

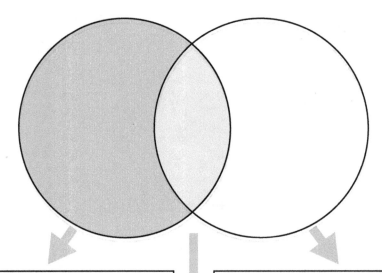

Color 1: If you were acting based on this aspect of your personality, how might you act, or what might you say?

Energy. I love board games and want to play them over and over and over. Also, I usually act very excited and cheer when good things happen.

Color 2: If you were acting based on this aspect of your personality, how might you act, or what might you say?

Hope. I act so anxious because I am hoping the game will turn out well. Every little move seems full of meaning and is the next step to hoped-for success, and I lean forward with anticipation.

Color Blending: If you were acting based on these two aspects of your personality blending together, how might you act, or what might you say?

I will probably continue to get on everyone's nerves, because I hope upon hope that someone, anyone, will play the game with me. My energy is such that I can never get enough, and I will keep asking everyone to play until they do! Then, when I am playing, I am hoping so much that I will win that I can pop out with cheering and dancing full of energy if I do. I suppose that is why it's sometimes hard to get anyone to play with me.

Lesson 5.5

Making Connections With Tangents

This lesson offers students a chance to work on a bit of geometry vocabulary as well as reflect on their lives a little more closely. This lesson emphasizes that no one is alone in this world. Yes, we do all make connections. Yes, there are others who are like us.

Materials

- » Handout 5.3: How Do You Feel About Colors?
- » Handout 5.5: Who's Your Tangent?
- » Handout 5.5: Who's Your Tangent? Sample
- » Compasses (one per student)
- » Rulers (one per student)

Estimated Time

- » 20 minutes

Procedure

Begin by having students complete Handout 5.5: Who's Your Tangent? *Tangent* is a term used in geometry to describe a straight line or plane that touches a curve at one point. Think of a ball sitting on top of a table. The table is a tangent to the ball. For this portion of the lesson, tangents take on a deeper meaning—that of connections our gifted learners feel with others. Students will consider their "tangents," or others who shares things in common with them, and then identify similarities among themselves and others. Sample answers can be found on the page following the handout.

Social and Emotional Curriculum for Gifted Students Grade 4

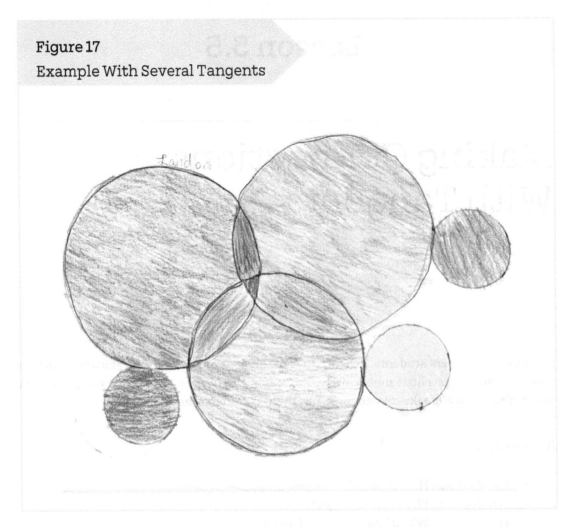

Figure 17
Example With Several Tangents

Once the activity sheet has been completed, display and review the color chart on Handout 5.3: How Do You Feel About Colors? Have students determine the proper color for their tangents. Then, using the overlapping circle drawings they have already created, students should use their compasses to draw a tangent to one of their circles—or perhaps several—in any size they choose (see Figure 17). In my classroom, one student wanted to know if it was OK to have more than one tangent—of course! Another approach is to draw tangents in size proportion to their importance.

I appreciate the opportunity this activity provides in knowing students a little better. Gifted students produce such amazing work that sometimes I forget they are just kids who want to have fun and be happy, run around, and feel lucky that they "found something they lost."

NAME: _____ DATE: _____

Handout 5.5

Who's Your Tangent?

Directions: Yes, there are others in the world who share things in common with you! Although no one is just like you, certainly others are your "tangents." Tangents are others who share things in common with you. Tangents don't have to be friends. They could be famous people, brothers or sisters, parents, or future friends you will meet someday. Identify one of your tangents and complete the following prompts about your similarities.

Things both you and your tangent might be thinking:

Things both you and your tangent might be doing:

Things others might say about both you and your tangent:

Things both you and your tangent might say:

Social and Emotional Curriculum for Gifted Students, Grade 4 © Prufrock Press Inc.

Handout 5.5: Who's Your Tangent? *continued*

Think and Discuss
The figure on the right represents a special sort of tangent in geometry. It's an *internal circular tangent*. If this figure is a metaphor for you and another person, explain what the internal circular tangent would represent about you and the other person. Share your ideas with the class.

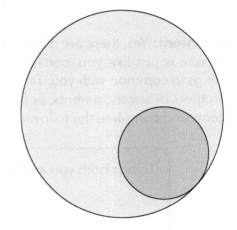

NAME:_____ DATE: _____

Handout 5.5

Who's Your Tangent? Sample

Directions: Yes, there are others in the world who share things in common with you! Although no one is just like you, certainly others are your "tangents." Tangents are others who share things in common with you. Tangents don't have to be friends. They could be famous people, brothers or sisters, parents, or future friends you will meet someday. Identify one of your tangents and complete the following prompts about your similarities.

> Things both you and your tangent might be thinking:
> *I hope the weather is nice enough to play soccer this weekend.*

> Things both you and your tangent might be doing:
> *We both might be practicing dribbling soccer balls around our houses and knocking things over—accidentally, of course!*

> Things others might say about both you and your tangent:
> *Those kids can't get enough soccer!*

> Things both you and your tangent might say:
> *When does the season start? What time is practice? Can I get new cleats? What time is the World Cup on today? How about we get a net for the backyard?*

Handout 5.5: Who's Your Tangent? Sample, *continued*

Think and Discuss
The figure on the right represents a special sort of tangent in geometry. It's an *internal circular tangent*. If this figure is a metaphor for you and another person, explain what the internal circular tangent would represent about you and the other person. Share your ideas with the class.

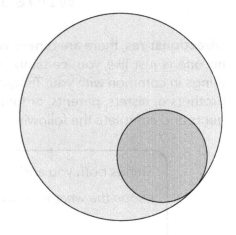

An internal tangent shows that we share ideas and feelings in common inside our hearts and minds. Internal tangents are people who are so alike us, they not only act like us, but they experience life like we do on the inside, too.

Lesson 5.6

What Color Is Giftedness?

You may have noticed that this unit has not yet covered the intersection of the three circles. It's altogether fitting and appropriate that our "center" in this lesson is *giftedness*. After all, don't all of our students share this characteristic?

Materials

- » Lesson 5.6: What Color Is Giftedness?
- » Lesson 5.6: What Color Is Giftedness? Sample
- » Overlapping circle drawings (see previous lessons)
- » Colored pencils

Estimated Time

- » 20 minutes

Procedure

Use Handout 5.6: What Color Is Giftedness? in a whole-class discussion of giftedness. Students will consider what they have learned about giftedness and select a color to represent the concept of giftedness. They will then fill in this color in the middle of their three overlapping circles. In my classroom, I let students decide which color they believe should represent giftedness. After all, although all students share being gifted learners, they all express this characteristic a little bit differently.

During this lesson, students should not only examine what giftedness is, but also what it *is not*. As always, students should back up their thoughts, opinions, and feelings with examples to best engage in critical thinking.

Encourage participation. Try to get as many voices into the room as possible. Some questions to consider during this lesson include:
- » Is giftedness the same for everyone?
- » Can you be gifted in more than one area?
- » Can you be gifted in areas that don't show up in school?
- » What *matters* when it comes to giftedness?
- » How can you tell if someone is a gifted learner?
- » Why do some people not want others to know they are gifted learners?
- » Is everyone gifted?

Follow-Up: Take-Home Activity

In this unit, students have created a physical metaphor that represents their personalities. Now that they have completed their overlapping circles, encourage students to take their drawings home and explain the components and the significance of the colors to their families.

NAME:_____ DATE: _____

Handout 5.6

What Color Is Giftedness?

Directions: Consider what you have learned and what you feel about different colors to answer the questions: What color is giftedness? What color is giftedness *not*? There are many right answers to these questions—including among experts in the field of gifted education. Be sure to explain why you think a color fits and to provide an example.

What color is giftedness?	What color is giftedness *not*?
Why?	Why?
Example:	Example:

UNIT 5: OUR COLORFUL SELVES

Social and Emotional Curriculum for Gifted Students, Grade 4 © Prufrock Press Inc.

NAME:_____ DATE: _____

Handout 5.6

What Color Is Giftedness? Sample

Directions: Consider what you have learned and what you feel about different colors to answer the questions: What color is giftedness? What color is giftedness *not*? There are many right answers to these questions—including among experts in the field of gifted education. Be sure to explain why you think a color fits and to provide an example.

What color is giftedness?	What color is giftedness *not*?
White.	Also white. Giftedness is not "exact."
Why? *Giftedness is "pure." It's not to say giftedness makes anyone more pure than anyone else. We are all pure because we are all who we are. Giftedness, for people who are gifted, is who they are.*	**Why?** *The directions say it best—there is no one exact definition for giftedness. "Exact" also could mean "perfection." Just because someone is gifted, it doesn't mean they are perfect. Far from it. Gifted people are human and make mistakes just like everyone else.*
Example: *Someone asks a simple question, and a gifted learner goes deep inside their mind to consider all kinds or different points of view, metaphors, and aspects to the question. They can't help it. It's who they are.*	**Example:** *My friend is amazing in math. I can write and read very well. Anna is an artist. Stuart is a fantastic athlete. Arturo can build almost anything. We are all gifted learners right here inside the same classroom, but there is no exact way we fit the many definitions of giftedness.*

Conclusion
Dear Gifted Learner

Collected in this section are various quotes and thoughts presented as short letters. Each is about life as a gifted learner in some way, and several are simply about life in general. Each letter opens discussion and allows students to pause and reflect in a mindful way—to slow down just a little bit and listen to their classmates' ideas and feelings.

I hope some of these letters inspire students to think ahead to all of the positive experiences they can build in their lives. A quote such as "Don't forget to wear a helmet" might at first bring looks of confusion. Doesn't this quote need more context? When this quote is shared and processed through the magic of metaphorical thinking in a classroom full of gifted kids, however, it can take on depth and power. "Don't forget to wear a helmet" may apply to many situations in life, not just riding a bike or snowboarding. How do we prepare? When and how should we protect ourselves—not just physically but also emotionally? When should we choose not to wear the metaphorical helmet?

I also hope some quotes, on the other hand, produce a little ire. "When are you going to start walking on water?" may raise some notes of indignation for your students, but it may just as well induce a little laughter. Indignation, ire, and laughter expressed in the safe atmosphere of your classroom lead to both engagement and impassioned discussion. Is this indignation felt because a student has felt unfair demands from others, or are perfectionists feeling an immediate frustrated feeling? Either way, engaging with these words spurs self-discovery—maybe not exactly in that moment, but perhaps somewhere down the line. Gifted learners can often see another's perspective very clearly, and reminders of some of the most important aspects of life (like "Breathe . . . much better. Thank you.") extend well beyond the classroom. In these ways, I hope these quotes and thoughts spur reflection, analysis, understanding, confluence, and some disagreement in a classroom climate that communicates acceptance and emotional safety. I hope everyone gets to hear some laughter, too.

These letters may be used as warm-ups with gifted students about once a week or so. Sometimes conversations may last 10 minutes, and sometimes 45 minutes. In my classroom, there have been times when we have returned to these discussions throughout the school year.

Thank you for taking care of our gifted learners.

NAGC Learning and Development Standards

1.1. Self-Understanding. Students with gifts and talents recognize their interests, strengths, and needs in cognitive, creative, social, emotional, and psychological areas.

1.2. Self-Understanding. Students with gifts and talents demonstrate understanding of how they learn and recognize the influences of their identities, cultures, beliefs, traditions, and values on their learning and behavior.

1.3. Self-Understanding. Students with gifts and talents demonstrate understanding of and respect for similarities and differences between themselves and their cognitive and chronological peer groups and others in the general population.

Themes and Skills Addressed

Social-Emotional Themes
- » Pride
- » Challenge
- » Identity
- » Executive functioning
- » What is giftedness?
- » Effort
- » Compassion
- » Empathy
- » Friendship
- » Resilience
- » Growth mindset

Dear Gifted Learner Letters Available Online

The Dear Gifted Learner Letters shared in this section may also be downloaded at https://www.prufrock.com/Social-and-Emotional-Curriculum-for-Gifted-Students-Resources.aspx.

Conclusion: Dear Gifted Learner

Academic Skills
» Collaborative discussion
» Inference

Dear Gifted Learner Letters

Dear gifted learner,

"Gifted learners should be right almost all of the time; otherwise, they are not gifted." Agree or disagree?

Sincerely,

_____

Social and Emotional Curriculum for Gifted Students, Grade 4 © Prufrock Press Inc.

Social and Emotional Curriculum for Gifted Students Grade 4

Dear gifted learner,

Great ability? Whatever.
Great opportunity? Now we're talking!

Sincerely,

_____

Social and Emotional Curriculum for Gifted Students, Grade 4 © Prufrock Press Inc.

Dear gifted learner,

We love quirky people! What quirks are you hiding from us?

Sincerely,

_____

Social and Emotional Curriculum for Gifted Students, Grade 4 © Prufrock Press Inc.

Conclusion: Dear Gifted Learner

Dear gifted learner,

The most important laughter is directed at yourself, but so is the most damaging. How can that be?

Sincerely,

_____

Social and Emotional Curriculum for Gifted Students, Grade 4 © Prufrock Press Inc.

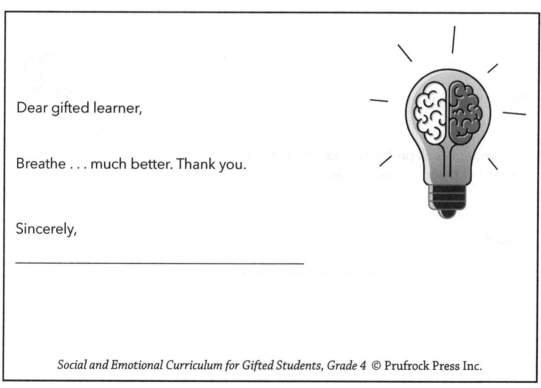

Dear gifted learner,

Breathe . . . much better. Thank you.

Sincerely,

_____

Social and Emotional Curriculum for Gifted Students, Grade 4 © Prufrock Press Inc.

Dear gifted learner,

A wise person once said, "Try and try again." An even wiser person didn't bother saying anything at all. They just lived it instead.

Sincerely,

_____

Social and Emotional Curriculum for Gifted Students, Grade 4 © Prufrock Press Inc.

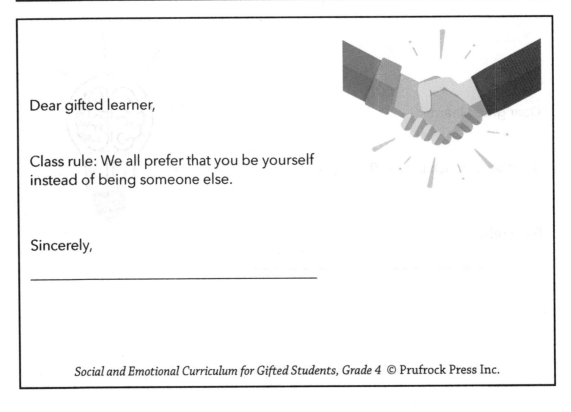

Dear gifted learner,

Class rule: We all prefer that you be yourself instead of being someone else.

Sincerely,

_____

Social and Emotional Curriculum for Gifted Students, Grade 4 © Prufrock Press Inc.

Conclusion: Dear Gifted Learner

Dear gifted learner,

I wonder how superheroes acted in fourth grade . . .

Sincerely,

_____

Social and Emotional Curriculum for Gifted Students, Grade 4 © Prufrock Press Inc.

Dear gifted learner,

It is so important to enjoy your successes and understand how hard you've worked for them. It is not so important to make sure you tell everyone about it.

Sincerely,

_____

Social and Emotional Curriculum for Gifted Students, Grade 4 © Prufrock Press Inc.

Social and Emotional Curriculum for Gifted Students Grade 4

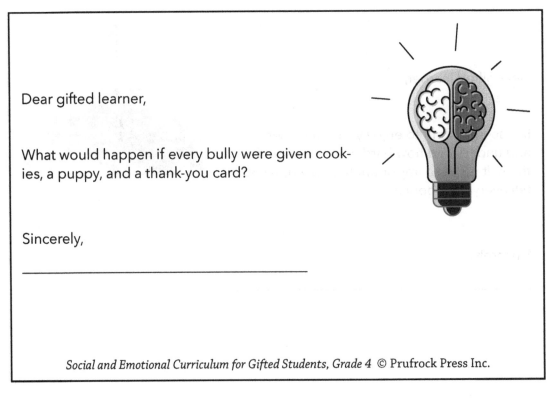

Dear gifted learner,

If you could choose only one tool to use for the rest of your days, what would it be?

Sincerely,

_____

Social and Emotional Curriculum for Gifted Students, Grade 4 © Prufrock Press Inc.

Dear gifted learner,

What would happen if every bully were given cookies, a puppy, and a thank-you card?

Sincerely,

_____

Social and Emotional Curriculum for Gifted Students, Grade 4 © Prufrock Press Inc.

Conclusion: *Dear Gifted Learner*

Dear gifted learner,

Don't forget to wear a helmet.

Sincerely,

_____

Social and Emotional Curriculum for Gifted Students, Grade 4 © Prufrock Press Inc.

Dear gifted learner,

It's OK to feel things very intensely. Now what will you do with those feelings?

Sincerely,

_____

Social and Emotional Curriculum for Gifted Students, Grade 4 © Prufrock Press Inc.

Dear gifted learner,

When was the last time you pressed a big red button? What happened?

Sincerely,

_____

Social and Emotional Curriculum for Gifted Students, Grade 4 © Prufrock Press Inc.

Dear gifted learner,

Where is your safe space?

Sincerely,

_____

Social and Emotional Curriculum for Gifted Students, Grade 4 © Prufrock Press Inc.

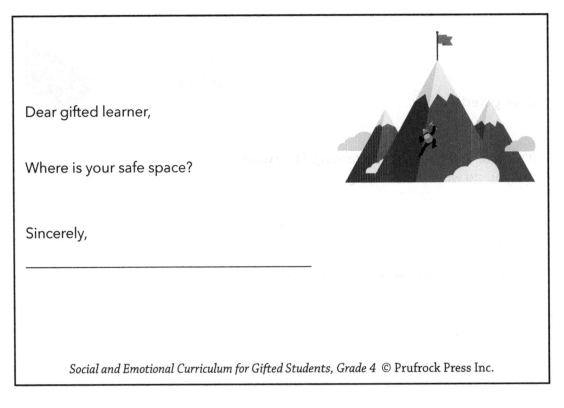

Conclusion: *Dear Gifted Learner*

Dear gifted learner,

You are excused from trying to solve all of the problems.

Sincerely,

_____

Social and Emotional Curriculum for Gifted Students, Grade 4 © Prufrock Press Inc.

Dear gifted learner,

Why haven't you started walking on water yet?

Sincerely,

_____

Social and Emotional Curriculum for Gifted Students, Grade 4 © Prufrock Press Inc.

Dear gifted learner,

Look around. Look inside. Look up and look down. While you are busy looking, make sure that you are *seeing*, too.

Sincerely,

_____

Social and Emotional Curriculum for Gifted Students, Grade 4 © Prufrock Press Inc.

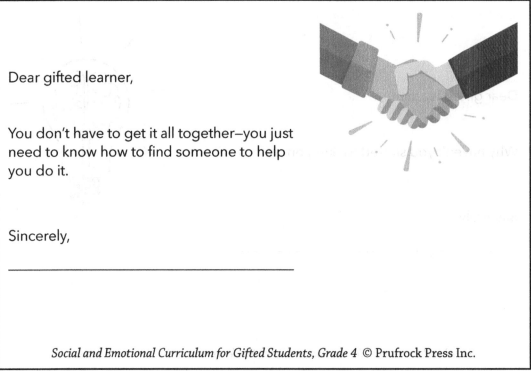

Dear gifted learner,

You don't have to get it all together—you just need to know how to find someone to help you do it.

Sincerely,

_____

Social and Emotional Curriculum for Gifted Students, Grade 4 © Prufrock Press Inc.

Conclusion: Dear Gifted Learner

Dear gifted learner,

You can't do everything. That would be so boring!

Sincerely,

_____

Social and Emotional Curriculum for Gifted Students, Grade 4 © Prufrock Press Inc.

Dear gifted learner,

Yes is the most powerful word in our language.

Sincerely,

_____

Social and Emotional Curriculum for Gifted Students, Grade 4 © Prufrock Press Inc.

References

Galbraith, J. (2009). *The gifted kids' survival guide*. Free Spirit.

National Association for Gifted Children. (2019). *2019 Pre-K–Grade 12 Gifted Programming Standards.* https://www.nagc.org/sites/default/files/standards/Intro%202019%20Programming%20Standards.pdf

Pyryt, M. (2004, June). Helping gifted students cope with perfectionism. *Parenting for High Potential*, 10–14.

Sumners, S., & Hines, M. E. (2020, August). Taking the creative leap: Thinking outside the "box." *Teaching for High Potential*, 19.

Sword, L. K. (2011). *Emotional intensity in gifted children*. Supporting the Emotional Needs of the Gifted. https://www.sengifted.org/post/emotional-intensity-in-gifted-children

About the Author

Mark Hess has spent more than 33 years teaching gifted learners. He is a gifted programs specialist in Colorado Springs, President-Elect for the Colorado Association for Gifted and Talented, and a member of the National Association for Gifted Children's advisory committee for *Teaching for High Potential* and NAGC's social-emotional needs committee. As a director on Supporting Emotional Needs of the Gifted's board, Mark is the senior associate editor of the SENG library. Visit Mark's website at https://www.giftedlearners.org to find free resources for parents and teachers to help meet the needs of gifted learners.